The New Administration's First 100 Days
Workbook

The New Administration's First 100 Days Workbook

TONY ROBINSON

Longman
New York • San Francisco • Boston
London • Toronto • Sydney • Tokyo • Singapore • Madrid
Mexico City • Munich • Paris • Cape Town • Hong Kong • Montreal

Editor-in-Chief: Eric Stano
Associate Development Editor: Donna Garnier
Executive Marketing Manager: Lindsey Prudhomme
Production Coordinator: Scarlett Lindsay
Cover Designer/Manager: John Callahan
Cover Illustration/Photo: Courtesy of Getty Images, Inc.
Senior Manufacturing Buyer: Alfred C. Dorsey
Printer and Binder: Courier Corporation / Stoughton
Cover Printer: Courier Corporation / Stoughton

Longman
is an imprint of

www.pearsonhighered.com

ISBN-13: 978-0-205-63942-7
ISBN-10:   0-205-63942-9

CONTENTS

Why do political observers obsess over the notion of the president's "First 100 Days"? Who invented the notion of the "First 100 Days," and has any president been able to match the president who started it all? You'll find out in exercise one.

Does the new president *truly* have a mandate to lead? Or do members of Congress and the media just think he does? See for yourself in exercise two.

Does the new president's budget propose to spend more money on guns or on butter? Research the answers in exercise five.

What does the rest of the world think about the new American president? Should Americans even care about global public opinion? Ponder the evidence in exercise seven.

Sometimes Congress is resistant to the president, and sometimes it just takes too long to get all the members of Congress to come to agreement. So what can a president do to achieve his goals and lead the nation without passing new laws? Learn for yourself in exercise eleven.

It's been eight years since America last inaugurated a new president, which makes spring of 2009 a time of portent and high drama. The new president faces immense challenges in stabilizing an economy, dealing with a planet grown skeptical of U.S. leadership, handling a "wolfpack" media, and negotiating with an often resistant Congress. These challenges tend to beat down even the most skilled of presidents. History shows that almost all presidents end their presidencies less popular and less powerful than when they began. This fact helps prove just how important the *beginning* of every new presidency is.

We call it the First 100 Days—those first three months of a new presidency, a "honeymoon period" when the public takes the measure of the man, when the media and Congress are least likely to call for the president's head, and when the president has a heightened ability to put his imprint on the politics of the day. The sense of national renewal and political possibility is never stronger than when a new president takes the stage to swear the oath of office—and from that moment on, the days tick away until the press and the scholars gather to assess just what the president achieved in his First 100 Days of office. What a president achieves during these First 100 Days—and how those days end up being assessed by the public, the media, and Congress—goes a long way to determining whether a new president will ultimately have great success over the next four years.

The First 100 Days of a new presidency is a dynamic and engaging time in American politics. With the innovative political "labs" in this book, you can be similarly dynamic and engaged as you follow these first months of the new president's term.

I would like to thank a few of those who played an important role in helping me to imagine and complete this book. The editorial staff at Pearson Longman, especially Donna Garnier and Scarlett Lindsay, were fantastic advisors and helped ensure a professional product. My wife, Minsun, my teenage daughter, Donalyn, and my two-year-old girl, Sora, are an inspiration and a joy and I thank them for all their patience and support.

I also must thank my parents, Butch and Donna Robinson, who gave me inspiration and confidence while growing up in the mountains of Montana, and to whom this small book is dedicated.

You are about to witness something rare and vitally important in American politics—the First 100 Days of a newly elected president. Since 1932, when the notion of the "First 100 Days" originated, it has only happened eleven other times. Though it happens rarely and is over quickly, it is often argued that the First 100 Days of a newly elected president play a vital role in shaping the political atmosphere for years afterward. You are fortunate, therefore, to be a student at this rare moment, able to dedicate serious attention to studying one of the most significant time periods in American politics.

President Franklin Roosevelt, taking office during an economic emergency and responding with a rapid array of new policies, crafted the notion of the "First 100 Days" of a presidency as a time for dramatic action and serious achievements. Ever since, every president has been evaluated by this standard: What did they achieve in their First 100 Days? It may be unfair, since no president has faced the same level of national emergency and subsequent national unity as Roosevelt did, but there is no denying that the First 100 Days frame will be used to judge the current president's success. And you will be able to watch it all unfold.

When you first open this book, America will be welcoming the first days of its new president; by the time you finish, the First 100 Days will be wrapping up. As a student of the First 100 Days, you will have an up-close view of one of the most exciting and meaningful time-periods in American politics—a period that offers a unique opportunity for memorable study and learning.

It is the goal of this book's collection of interactive exercises (you could call them political science "labs") to guide you in personally engaging the First 100 Days of the new president's term, and to open up an exciting world of firsthand political research. This is no textbook. We all know that sometimes textbooks can be dry and even boring, and that it's not always easy to learn and remember the lessons encountered in chapter after chapter of passive reading. As a supplement to the typical textbook, this book takes a different approach. Here, you will learn about politics through hands-on interactive exercises, viewing video clips, visiting unique websites, and opening powerful databases. Though standard textbooks and traditional methods of study are vital, *students often learn best by doing*—by actively engaging course materials, by interacting with various data sets, and by experiencing information in multiple mediums. That's what this book is all about.

Through interactive exercises, this book guides you in locating and utilizing some of the best political resources on the Web. The exercises parallel the unfolding events of the First 100 Days, allowing you to learn about events as they happen. As you watch current news clips, for example, this workbook will guide you in understanding how current reporting compares with historic assessments of different presidential transitions. You may have heard about FDR's First 100 Days. Through this workbook, you will view some of the images and reporting from that famous period first-hand. You will also learn how to research presidential budget priorities, global public opinion polls, and the subject of often obscure—but politically crucial—executive orders and agreements.

Throughout these exercises, you will have the opportunity to compare the current president's leadership to that of presidents throughout history. Why is FDR remembered as such a successful president, which have been the greatest inaugural addresses, and does the current president measure up to the standards of the past? Learn how to evaluate such things by looking at the record of history, exploring the president's "batting average" with Congress, reading over public opinion polls, and more.

The exercises are fun, but serious, political lessons.

- Each exercise is introduced by a short theoretical overview.

- The exercises are presented in step-by-step fashion, guiding you with internet links to some of the best resources on the Web and advice on how to use the wealth of information at each site.

- Frequent screenshots of what you will be seeing on the Internet are provided, so that you can always be confident that you are at the right place.

- Each exercise is followed by an attached worksheet, on which you can report your findings as you move through the exercise.

Throughout these exercises, you will be learning a bit of what it means to be a political scientist—exploring databases, evaluating political events as they unfold, and comparing today's events to important moments in history. When done, you will have encountered, evaluated, and produced substantial first-hand knowledge about American politics. You will have mastered the events of the First 100 Days—everything from evaluating the presidential inaugural to measuring his success rate in Congress. You will have experienced the birth of a presidency that you won't soon forget.

To help you make the most of this workbook, here are some tips:

- The exercises are built around Internet resources. Though the websites in this book are generally stable and predictable, there is always the chance that some links will have become broken, some websites will change, etc. All such changes will be monitored by the author of this book, and updates and corrections to every exercise will be posted regularly at www.pearsonhighered.com/robinson1e. **Before you begin any exercise, you should go to www.pearsonhighered.com/robinson1e, click the button for the relevant exercise, and note any updates or corrections.**

- Each exercise is followed by a worksheet. As you move through the exercise, you will be instructed at various points to fill in your answers and thoughts on the worksheet. It is best to detach the worksheet before you begin the exercise and to fill it in step-by-step, as you move through the exercise itself.

- At www.pearsonhighered.com/robinson1e, you can find downloadable versions of all worksheets. These downloadable worksheets will allow you to type your information into the worksheet on your computer and expand your ideas as much as desired, without being bound to the space limitations of hard-copy worksheets in this book.

- As you move through each exercise, you will note that links you are to follow or places you are to click on a webpage are always printed in **bold font.** Whenever you see **bold font,** you should note that you are being asked to perform an action on a webpage.

- When you are instructed to fill in your worksheet, the directions are *printed in italics.* Whenever you see *italicized font,* you should note that you are being asked to complete a step in the worksheet.

- Throughout the exercises, you will type various web addresses into your browser. It is easy to make mistakes in typing addresses— so whenever a page doesn't load correctly, you should double-check to be sure you typed the address correctly. If you wish to avoid typing all these addresses by hand, you can visit www.pearsonhighered.com/robinson1e to find an electronic list of ALL the hyperlinks, organized by chapter. You can use this list of links to simply click on each relevant hotlink when the workbook instructs you to, or to cut and paste the links into your browser.

- Following the exercises, there is a section of reflection questions to guide further thinking on the subject. Your teacher might use these questions to stimulate classroom discussion on the themes in these exercises.

Enough preliminaries;

turn the page to experience the First 100 Days!

TO THE INSTRUCTOR

This book is meant to supplement your teaching in American politics and presidency courses. It provides a set of hands-on political science "labs," built around the unfolding events of the First 100 Days of the new president's term. The exercises build on my own insights as a long-time teacher of American politics, and the recent success I have found in utilizing rapidly exploding internet resources to study events as they unfold in real time.

Though events like the First 100 Days of a new presidency are naturally exciting and are terrific teaching opportunities, teachers know that any subject can be enlivened with hands-on opportunities for students, multimedia instructional aides, and opportunities for independent student discovery. It's no surprise that students often learn best by doing—by active engagement in exploring, evaluating and creating political knowledge. We also know that the Web can be a great resource in facilitating this independent exploration—but that it is also a crowded, chaotic and noisy place, full of junk as well as jewels. It is sometimes hard to know where to direct students for the best and most reliable research. This book helps teachers cut through the clutter of the Web and catalyzes student learning by guiding them through active exploration of high quality internet resources,

The workbook is organized into twelve exercises, each built around an issue that parallels the events of the First 100 Days. If completed on a weekly basis throughout the spring term, the exercises are generally organized to parallel the calendar of the First 100 Days (i.e., early exercises assess whether there was an election mandate and evaluate the inaugural address, whereas later events focus on the president's success rate with Congress). In many cases, instructors may want to move the exercises around a bit and skip some altogether. In general, there will be no problem in assigning exercises in whatever order desired—but you should be aware that the second half of the exercises fit far better into the later days of the First 100 days, while the first half should be assigned earlier.

Each exercise should take students 1.5 to 2 hours to complete. A lot depends on how interested students become in exploring the rich website material they will encounter, beyond what is necessary to complete the exercise. Each exercise provides a theoretical framing of each issue, helping students to connect the practical exercises with deeper meanings.

It is unavoidable that students may encounter broken links or a few changed websites as they work through these exercises. The author will constantly monitor exercises for such problems, and updates, corrections and solutions will be posted at www.pearsonhighered.com/robinson1e. Before students begin each exercise, they should go to this site and click the button for the relevant exercise for all such information. A complete list of all hyperlinks, organized by chapter, is available at this website as well, so students can download this file and use hotlinks to all the links referenced in the workbook, if they choose.

There are many ways to use the exercises in this book. Ideas include:

- A ready-made set of hands-on, out-of-classroom assignments, to supplement regular classroom and textbook learning.

- Enhanced classroom discussions as students come with their own insights based on their learning in these labs. Discussion questions at the end of the workbook can also help stimulate discussion.

- Students can build on what they learn to produce research projects of their own, using the Web resources they have encountered here.

- The text will help students to become "amateur" political scientists, drawing on some of the same data and resources that scholars use in their research. Students will be introduced to some of the basics of producing and evaluating political knowledge on their own.

- Introducing the teacher to a wealth of quality internet resources and strategies for teaching American politics more effectively.

The New Administration's First 100 Days
Workbook

Franklin Delano Roosevelt was inaugurated in 1933 in the midst of the Great Depression—America's greatest economic challenge in history. Thousands of banks had failed, 25% of the nation was unemployed, and one-third of the nation was "ill-housed, ill-clad, ill-nourished" (to quote FDR in his second Inaugural Address). Facing challenges like no other president, FDR adopted a vigorous course of action to pull America out of crisis during his "First 100 Days" as president. Ever since, political observers have expected great things out of the president during the "First 100 Days," and have judged initial presidential success by this benchmark.

FDR set the bar for future presidential success very high during his First 100 Days. On his very first day in office, March 4, 1933, FDR called Congress into special session. He proceeded to lead Congress to pass several bills that reformed the banking industry, offered Americans immediate Depression relief payments, reshaped American agriculture and kick-started industrial recovery with substantial federal investment.

During those First 100 Days, FDR also used executive orders to create the Civilian Conservation Corps, the Public Works Administration, the Rural Electrification Administration and the Tennessee Valley Authority. These projects put thousands of Americans back to work building dams, bridges, highways and public utility systems—all at decent wages.

By the time Congress adjourned its special session on June 16, 1933, the foundation of Roosevelt's economic agenda (called the "New Deal") was in place. America was on its way to ending the Great Depression.

Ever since, presidents have been judged by the energy and success of their First 100 Days in office. In general, presidents enjoy high levels of public support during this time, and Congress is more likely to defer to and support presidential leadership. We call this the "honeymoon" period of the new presidency—a time of good will when a president can most effectively imprint his will upon the American political system, shaping the political landscape for the following four years.

It may be a bit unfair to compare recent presidents to the historic leadership of FDR during a time of great national crisis—but there is no denying that it happens. Presidential historian Doris Kearns Goodwin has noted that:

> Every president since Franklin Roosevelt wishes that the term '100 days' could be exorcised from the language. I mean, in some ways it's so unfair to compare that extraordinary accomplishment in the time of crisis when the country needed presidential action with ordinary presidents in ordinary times.[1]

How did FDR create the concept of the "First 100 Days," and how has the concept organized our understanding of presidents through history? In this exercise, you will review some of the events of the very first "First 100 Days," during FDR's presidency. You will review how presidents such as Nixon, Reagan, Clinton and Bush have all been judged by the "success" of their own "First 100 Days." An understanding of how this important concept has been used throughout history will help you come to a better understanding and evaluation of how the concept is being used this year to frame public understanding of the current presidency. How does the current president's First 100 Days compare to presidents throughout history? Should we focus so much on this artificial timeline in judging presidential success?

---

[1] Doris Kearns Goodwin, "The First 100 Days." *PBS Newshour with Jim Lehrer.* April 30, 2001. www.pbs.org/newshour/bb/white_house/jan-june01/100days_4-30.html (Accessed September 30, 2008).

THE FIRST 100 DAYS IN PRESIDENTIAL HISTORY

1. You will begin your study of the First 100 Days throughout history by reviewing some of the details of how the very first of the First 100 Days unfolded under Franklin Roosevelt. The Franklin D. Roosevelt Presidential Library and Museum has organized an exhibition of FDR's First 100 Days. To see some of it, go to **www.fdrlibrary. marist.edu/100home.html**.

2. You see the homepage of the First 100 Days exhibit, including a poster advertising FDR's call for progress in 1933: "Action and Action Now." To see more of the exhibit, click the **"Introduction" link** on the bottom of the page.

EXHIBITION HOME | INTRODUCTION | EXHIBITION FLYER | EVENTS | RESOURCES

3. After reading the short summary of the challenges facing FDR on the introduction page, click the link for **"Exhibition Flyer,"** which is on both the top and bottom of the Introduction screen.

4. You are taken to a pdf file with a number of interesting images from the First 100 Days exhibition. Look over these images and read the short text that accompanies them. You will learn more about the challenges facing FDR and the quick policy responses adopted by FDR and Congress.

5. To address the challenges of his time, FDR called a special session of Congress to order. Over the next 100 days, FDR worked with Congress to pass a dramatic set of economic reforms known as the New Deal. These reforms created unprecedented government involvement in the operation of the nation's economy and became the foundation of the Democratic Party's new governing philosophy. You can learn about the speed with which these reforms were implemented by going to **www.voanews.com/specialenglish/archive/2006-08/ 2006-08-30-voa2.cfm.** Here you can listen to a Voice of America radio broadcast summarizing the month by month progress of Roosevelt's First 100 Days, or read the transcript of the broadcast.

6. Finally, you can see an interesting short video about the early days of the FDR presidency as part of the PBS "American Experience" series on the presidents. Go to **www.pbs.org/wgbh/amex/presidents/ video/fdr_01_wm.html#v102.** Here you can view the video "Above All, Try Something," or read the transcript of the video. You only need to watch about the first half of the video, up to the section where the focus shifts from FDR's First 100 Days to a focus on Eleanor Roosevelt.

7. What were some specific challenges faced by FDR through the First 100 Days of his presidency and how did he respond? *Based on what you have learned in the previous steps, describe a few of those specific challenges and responses on the worksheet.*

8. FDR's legendary First 100 Days have shaped how all subsequent presidents have been judged in the media, by scholars, and by the public. For an example of how the "First 100 Days" frame is used to

analyze a presidency, go to **www.time.com/time/magazine/article/0,9171,840053-1,00.html** and review how Time Magazine covered the Nixon presidency in 1969.

9. Franklin Roosevelt is remembered as leading the most successful presidency of the last 75 years, and the policies of his First 100 Days created much of the world Americans still live in. Since those days, the only president commonly compared to FDR in the sweeping way he reshaped the American political landscape was Ronald Reagan, who served from 1981–1988. Reagan brought what is called the "Reagan Revolution" to American politics. The next several steps explore the First 100 Days of the "Reagan Revolution."

10. To view some of the events of the First 100 Days of the Reagan Revolution, go to the PBS website built around the film "Reagan": **www.pbs.org/wgbh/amex/reagan/timeline/index_3.html**.

TIMELINE OF

RONALD REAGAN'S LIFE

1911-1958 ◀	1983-1985
1959-1977	1986-1988
1978-1982	1989-2000

1911   **February 6:** Ronald Wilson Reagan is born in Tampico, Illinois, the second of two sons to John (Jack) and Nelle Reagan.

1920   After years of moving from town to town, the Reagan family settles in Dixon, Illinois.

1922   **September 21:** Reagan is baptized at his mother's Disciples of Christ Church.

11. To see the events of Reagan's First 100 Days in this timeline, **scroll down the timeline to January 20, 1981**. This was Inauguration Day, the first day of Reagan's administration. You may have to click the button for the "1978–1982" period (at the top of the screen) to call up the appropriate section of the timeline.

12. **Read over the timeline events that fall between January 20, 1981 and April 28, 1981**—a period of time roughly paralleling the First 100 Days of the Reagan administration. As you study the timeline, keep in mind that Reagan is remembered for having brought a "Reagan Revolution" to American politics. What events from the timeline seem particularly memorable, important or revolutionary to you?

13. After you have reviewed the timeline, go to **www.pbs.org/ wgbh/amex/presidents/video/reagan_10_wm.html#v138**. On this website, you can view the Reagan section of the PBS video series on the American Presidents. **View the video clip you see here, and/or read the transcript that is right below it.**

14. Based on the information you have reviewed in the previous two steps, why do you think people say that Reagan brought a revolution to American politics? *On your worksheet, summarize one important achievement or new policy direction that the "Reagan Revolution" brought to America in his First 100 Days.*

15. Now you will look at the First 100 Days of more recent presidents. The PBS NewsHour with Jim Lehrer has built a website around analyzing the First 100 Days of George H.W. Bush, Bill Clinton and George W. Bush.

16. Go to **www.pbs.org/newshour/media/100days**. You will see options to explore the First 100 Days of several recent presidents. **Begin by following the link for "Gergen and Shields" on "George Bush's First 100 Days"** (see screenshot).

President Bush's First 100 Days
An Online NewsHour Special Report

'Hundred Days' History
The NewsHour's panel of historians examines how past presidents have measured up at their hundred day mark. (4/30/01)

Political Perspective
Political analysts Mark Shields and Paul Gigot and pollster Andrew Kohut examine the first 100 days of the Bush Administration. (4/27/01)

The President and the Press
Examining Mr. Bush's early relationship with the press. (4/25/01)
Extended Interview: Spokesman Ari Fleischer

The Bush Administration: Major Issues and Milestones

Bush/Cheney Transition | Address to Congress | Tax Cut Debate | Standoff with China

Bill Clinton's
First 100 Days

- Political Views
- Pollsters & Analysts
- Gergen & Shields
- Issues & Milestones

George Bush's
First 100 Days

Gergen & Shields
Issues & Milestones

17. *After viewing the Gergen and Shields video, or reading the transcript, fill in the worksheet with a few sentences describing the overall tone or key event(s) of the First 100 Days of the George H.W. Bush presidency.*

18. Return to **www.pbs.org/newshour/media/100days** and click on the link for **"Pollsters and Analysts"** in the section of the webpage dedicated to "Bill Clinton's First 100 Days."

19. *After viewing the video found here, or reading the transcript, fill in the worksheet with a few sentences describing the overall tone or key event(s) of the First 100 Days of the Clinton presidency.*

20. Now you can review the coverage of the most recent president, George W. Bush. Return to **www.pbs.org/newshour/media/100days**. Click the link for **"Political Perspective"** in the **"President Bush's First 100 Days"** Section (see screenshot). Watch or read the coverage you find there.

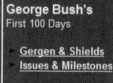

the web site of The NewsHour with Jim Lehrer

Online NewsHour

President Bush's First 100 Days
An Online NewsHour Special Report

'Hundred Days' History
The NewsHour's panel of historians examines how past presidents have measured up at their hundred day mark (4/30/01)

Political Perspective
Political analysts Mark Shields and Paul Gigot and pollster Andrew Kohut examine the first 100 days of the Bush Administration. (4/27/01)

The President and the Press
Examining Mr. Bush's early relationship with the press. (4/25/01)
Extended Interview: Spokesman Ari Fleischer

The Bush Administration: Major Issues and Milestones

Bush/Cheney Transition | Address to Congress | Tax Cut Debate | Standoff with China

Bill Clinton's
First 100 Days

- Political Views
- Pollsters & Analysts
- Gergen & Shields
- Issues & Milestones

George Bush's
First 100 Days

- Gergen & Shields
- Issues & Milestones

21. CNN also maintains a web resource on the First 100 Days of the George W. Bush presidency. You can access it at **www.cnn.com/SPECIALS/2001/bush.100/**.

22. When this page loads, you will see numerous links you can explore for more information on the early days of the George W. Bush presidency, including links for news stories (such as "Making the presidency his own"), a video calendar and timeline, and even a link to a CNN

pundits" report card (see screenshot). Explore some of these links to help round out your evaluation of the First 100 Days of the Bush presidency.

23. *Based on what you learned in the previous three steps, use the worksheet to summarize at least one aspect of the tone, style or policies of the First 100 Days of the George W. Bush presidency.*

24. Now that you have reviewed several "First 100 Days" through history, you are better situated to understand exactly why political observers tend to use this frame and you can draw conclusions about whether it is a useful standard for understanding and evaluating a president's early days. Before you offer your final analysis on this question, view a set of presidential scholars talking over just this question. Go to

www.pbs.org/newshour/bb/white_house/jan-june01/100days_4-30.html. View the "First 100 Days" video that you find there and/or read the transcript.

25. In the news video you just reviewed, journalist Haynes Johnson claims that the idea of the First 100 Days is "a foolish standard to apply to any president." What do you think? What is useful about analyzing a president through the lens of the First 100 Days, and what is foolish about such a frame? *On the worksheet, describe why you find the "First 100 Days" frame to be either a useful or foolish way to examine the unfolding leadership of the new president.*

Done!

THE FIRST 100 DAYS IN PRESIDENTIAL HISTORY

1. What were some specific challenges faced by FDR through the First 100 Days of his presidency and how did he respond?

2. Summarize one important achievement or new policy direction that the "Reagan Revolution" brought to America in his First 100 Days.

3. Provide a few sentences describing the overall tone or key event(s) of the First 100 Days of the George H.W. Bush presidency

4. Describe the tone or key event(s) of the First 100 Days under Clinton.

5. Briefly describe the tone, style or policies of the First 100 Days of the George W. Bush Presidency.

6. Explain why you find the "First 100 Days" frame to be either a useful or foolish way to examine the leadership of the new president.

ISSUE TWO:
WAS THERE A MANDATE?

Did the winner of the 2008 presidential election receive a "mandate" to lead from the voters? "No concept invokes the connection between the public and the president more than the electoral mandate, for it implies that the president shall work to make the will of the people into law."[1] Frequently, presidential election victors claim a "mandate" from the people to implement specific policies and to lead Congress in general. For example, on election night 1980, the vice-president-elect claimed that Ronald Reagan's victory was

> "not simply a mandate for change, but a mandate for peace and freedom; a mandate for prosperity; a mandate for opportunity for all Americans . . . a mandate to make government the servant of the people in the way our founding fathers intended; . . . a mandate for hope of fulfillment of the great dream that President-elect Reagan has worked for all his life."[2]

President Bush celebrated his 2004 victory with similar claims:

> "... when you win, there is a feeling that the people have spoken and embraced your point of view . . . the people made it clear what they wanted . . . I've earned capital in this camp and now I intend to use it . . . I'm going to spend it for what I told the people I'd spend it on, which is—you've heard the agenda: Social Security and tax reform, moving this economy forward, education, fighting and winning the war on terror."[3]

---

[1] Patricia Heidotting Conley, *Presidential Mandates: How Elections Shape the National Agenda* (Chicago: University of Chicago Press, 2001), p. 1.
[2] Quoted in Robert Dahl, "Myth of the Presidential Mandate," *Political Science Quarterly* 105 (1990): p 355.
[3] President Bush, "President Holds Press Conference," www.whitehouse.gov/news/releases/2004/11/20041104-5.html (accessed November 4, 2007).

Many scholars are skeptical of the idea of a "presidential mandate." How can there be a mandate for specific policies, when voters are usually ignorant about the policy goals of candidates, campaigns are driven by simplistic 30 second ads, and the results of the election are usually "noisy and ambiguous as signals of the electorate's concerns and intentions"?[4]

Still others point out that it doesn't really matter whether or not voters truly meant to support a specific "mandate" for change. Even if voters aren't informed and united enough to support a specific agenda, leaders in Congress and across the land often *believe* that voters support the president-elect's policies. If other politicians act on their perceptions of a mandate by supporting the president's policies, then it is same as if the mandate were a real fact.[5]

Claims of a presidential mandate, therefore, are important. If a mandate truly exists, it allows voters to express their desires through presidential leadership, who can push forward policies desired by the people. And whether or not voters are united behind a presidential mandate, presidents often claim they are. When politicians and pundits rally around these claims, it helps the president to advance his policies.

But not all elections are interpreted by politicians and pundits as delivering a mandate. Some elections, like FDR's 1932 victory and Reagan's 1980 victory, are widely seen as delivering a clear message from the voters—while many others are seen only as politics as usual. Did the 2008 election deliver a historic mandate to the presidential victor, or is it best seen as just another normal presidential election? You will explore that question in this exercise by examining: the scope of the president's election victory, congressional election results, key voter groups and policy issues in the election, and the "conventional wisdom" among the pundits and the press—do they *think* a mandate was delivered?

---

[4] Conley, p. 23.

[5] Lawrence J. Grossback, et. al., "Comparing Competing Theories on the Causes of Mandate Perceptions," *American Journal of Political Science* 49 (2005): 406-419.

WAS THERE A MANDATE?

1. Many scholars point out that mandates emerge when several conditions occur. These conditions include:

   - The president's scope of victory is strong (i.e., the president wins by a large margin)

   - The president's party registers strong gains in Congress

   - New voter groups emerge in dramatic fashion (or shifting loyalties transform existing voting groups)

   - Policy signals from voters are strong and clear

   - Among the press and officials, a consensus or "conventional wisdom" emerges that the president has won a mandate

   In this exercise, you will explore whether these conditions were present in the 2008 election.

2. Begin by examining the president's scope of victory. For an election to be considered a mandate, the size of the president's victory must be large, compared to other elections. You can examine the size of victories in previous elections by going to **www.presidency.ucsb.edu**.

3. You are now at "The American Presidency Project" of John Woolley and Gerhard Peters of the University of California at Santa Barbara. If you click on the "**elections**" button in the menu at the top of the page, you see a list of election years that you can explore, calling up maps and other data for various election years, if you wish.

4. You can also see a comprehensive list of data from *all* presidential elections by clicking on the "**data**" button, as in the screenshot on the next page. Do that now.

5. You are taken to a list of data archives related to the presidency. For this exercise, you are interested in the archive on **"Popular and Electoral Vote Mandates,"** which is in the **"Presidential Selection"** section of the page. Scroll down the page to select this link.

Growth of the Executive Branch
- ◆ Federal Budget Receipts and Outlays
- ◆ Differences in Appropriations Proposed by P[...]s
- ◆ Executive Orders
- ◆ White House Staff Budget
- ◆ Size of the Executive Office of the President

> Click here for data on the size of various election victories

Presidential Selection
- ◆ Popular and Electoral Vote Mandates
- ◆ Representation of President's Party in House Elections
- ◆ Voter Turnout in Presidential Elections
- ◆ Election Year Presidential Preferences Over Time
- ◆ Financing Presidential General Elections
- ◆ % of Convention Delegates Selected through Primary Elections Democratic | R[...]

6. After clicking on the link, you are taken to charts showing the size of election victories through history. Study these charts to get a sense of several "landslide" victories that are widely regarded as delivering popular mandates, versus other elections that are not interpreted this way. Particularly examine the data in the following elections, which have all been argued to have delivered popular mandates:

   - Franklin Roosevelt's 1932 and 1936 elections
   - Lyndon Johnson's 1964 election
   - Richard Nixon's 1972 election
   - Ronald Reagan's 1980 and 1984 elections

7. The raw data on this webpage has been converted by this workbook's author into a graph (below), which tracks the **"electoral vote advantage"** of presidential winners through history. As you can see in the graph (which compares the percentage of all electoral votes captured by the winning candidate to those captured by the loser), there is a real difference between the landslide or "mandate" elections (circled in the screenshot below) and other elections.

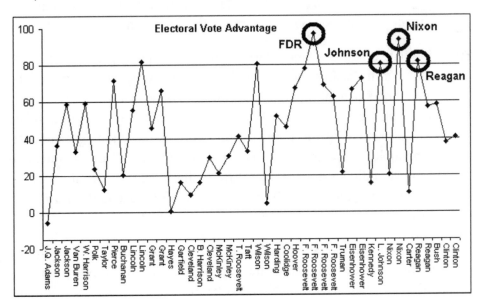

8. To help you determine whether the 2008 presidential victory was a historically unusual "mandate" election similar to these other landslide elections, you need to determine the average size of "normal" popular vote and electoral college victories, and the average size of "mandate election" victories—so that you can compare the two. For the purposes of this exercise, the calculations on the historical data have already been done for you. Here are the results.

	Normal Election	Mandate Election
Popular Vote Advantage*	5.4%	16.6%
Percent of Electoral Votes*	66%	94%

Popular Vote Advantage = Percent of all popular votes won by the winning candidate MINUS the percent of popular votes won by the loser.

Percent of Electoral Votes = Percent of all Electoral College votes won by the winning candidate.

9. Now that you know how "normal" election margins compare to "mandate" elections, you can compare the data to the 2008 results.

10. Using data on the 2008 popular vote breakdown that you can find with a basic internet search, determine the "Popular Vote Advantage" of the winning presidential candidate in 2008. You can do this by simply subtracting the percent of the popular vote won by the losing candidate from the percent of the popular vote won by the winning candidate. For example, if "Winning Candidate A" received 54% of the vote, and "Losing Candidate B" received 46% of the vote, you would subtract 46 from 54 to come up with an 8% Popular Vote Advantage. *Fill this information into your worksheet.*

11. Now determine the percent of all Electoral College votes won by the winning presidential candidate in 2008. You do this by simply dividing all the Electoral College votes won by the winning candidate by the total number of electoral colleges existing (538). For example, if the winning candidate won 300 electoral votes, you would divide

300 by 538 and come up with .557, or 55.7%. *Determine your answer and fill in the information on the worksheet.*

12. On the worksheet, you can see how the numbers from the 2008 election compare to the historical data from "normal" elections and to the data from unusual "landslide" or "mandate" elections. Based just on this comparison, does the 2008 election meet the standards for a mandate election or not? *Fill in the answer on your worksheet.*

13. The scale of the presidential victory in the popular vote and Electoral College is just one way to measure a presidential mandate. Another measure is the scale of the gains made by the president's party in Congress. If the president's party gained many seats in Congress, the election is more likely to be called a mandate.

14. To determine if the number of congressional seats gained or lost by the president's party in the 2008 election is historically unusual, you need to determine the average number of seats gained in Congress by the president's party in historical "mandate" elections versus the average number of seats gained for the president's party in "normal" elections. Because only one-third of Senate seats turn over each election, you will only examine turnover in the House of Representatives.

15. The historical numbers you need have already been calculated for you in this exercise, according to the following assumptions. "Mandate" elections in modern times are assumed to be Franklin Roosevelt in 1932 and 1936, Lyndon Johnson in 1964, Richard Nixon in 1972, and Ronald Reagan in 1980 and 1984. **The average number of House seats gained by the president-elect's party in these "mandate" elections was 39. In all other presidential elections since 1932, the average number of House seats gained by the president-elect's party was 8.**

16. *Though you don't have to complete this step for this exercise*, you may view the data utilized to determine the figures in step 14 by going to **http://en.wikipedia.org/wiki/Elections in the United States**. A good

database of historic election data is maintained here. Scroll down the page and you will see links to data from every congressional election (see screenshot).

United States presidential elections
)	1824	1828	1832	1836	1840	1844	1848	1852	1856	1860	1864	1868	1872	1876	1880	1884	8	1940	1944	1948	1952	1956	1960	1964	1968	1972	1976	1980	1984	1988	1992	1996	2000	

See also: House | Senate | Governors

United States House of Representatives Elections
+	1806	1808	1810	1812	1814	1816	1818	1820	1822	1824	1826	1828	1830	1832	1834	1836	)	1872	1874	1876	1878	1880	1882	1884	1886	1888	1890	1892	1894	1896	1898	1900	1902	8	1938	1940	1942	1944	1946	1948	1950	1952	1954	1956	1958	1960	1962	1964	1966	1968	1986	1988	1990	1992	1994	1996	1998	2000	2002	2004	2006	*2008*	Special

See also: Senate | President | Governors

17. Now that you know the average number of House seats gained by the president-elect's party in a "mandate" election (39) and the average seats gained in a "normal" election (8), you can determine whether the number of House seats gained (or lost) by the president-elect in the 2008 election can be considered evidence of a mandate or not.

18. Using any source, determine how many seats the president-elect's party gained or lost in the House of Representatives in 2008. *Report this number on your worksheet, and add your assessment of whether this data suggests a presidential mandate or not.*

19. Another important aspect of judging whether an election delivered a mandate from the voters is to determine whether important voter groups emerged to influence the election. For example, if lower-income voters or younger voters voted far more heavily than usual, and overwhelmingly voted for the winning candidate, it could be said that these voters were delivering a mandate for new policies that would benefit them.

20. To identify important voter groups and explore whether they were delivering a mandate for presidential leadership, you can explore "exit poll" data. Exit polling data is generated when thousands of voters are asked who they voted for and why, as they leave the voting both.

Sophisticated formulas guide the selection of voters and interpretation of the results, so that we can be fairly confident that the exit poll results actually reflect the viewpoints of voters in general. What do the 2008 exit polling data show?

21. CNN maintains a good database of exit poll data from recent presidential elections. To help you put the 2008 exit polling data in perspective, you can begin by viewing some of the data from the 2004 election. This will help you better understand recent patterns and to detect substantial changes (if any) that have occurred since then.

22. You can review the 2004 exit polling data at the CNN archives. Go to **www.cnn.com/ELECTION/2004/pages/results/states/US/P/00/.** You will see a link to find the full exit poll data to the right of this page. Click on "**voter survey results**" as in the screenshot below.

	STILL VOTING	PROCESSING RESULTS	TOO CLOSE TO CALL	PARTY CONTROL CHANGED	COUNTY MAP	**PARTY KEY**

Full President ›

CANDIDATE	VOTE	VOTE %	PRECINCTS	LOCAL	EXIT POLLS
R **Bush** (Incumbent)	62,040,606	51%	100% of precincts reporting	not available	voter survey results
D **Kerry**	59,028,109	48%			
I **Nader**	411,304	1%			

Screenshot: www.cnn.com

23. The exit poll data from 2004 appears. As you scroll through the data, you can see how different categories of voters broke down in terms of

whether they were heavily Bush (Republican) or Kerry (Democrat), or whether they were balanced. There are tips on how to read the data.

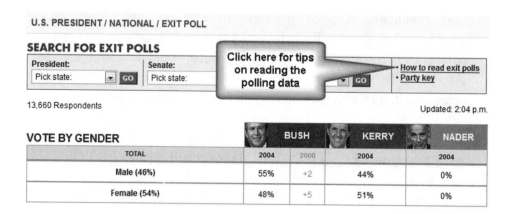

24. The first column of data (i.e., the column that has headers like "vote by gender," or "vote by race and gender") contains categories of voters (such as "White Men" or "White Women"). Each category is followed by a percentage, such as "White Men (36%)." The percentage figure is the number of all voters polled who were within that specific category—for example, 36% of all voters polled were white men. That gives you a sense of how large each voter category is.

25. Spend some time exploring the categories of voters that this data provides and analyzing how different groups voted.

26. Based on this exploration, determine one group of voters that was a large percent of the electorate and that was a key voting bloc for Bush, showing significantly more support for the Republican candidate than for Kerry. For example, if you scroll down the webpage you can see that 43% of all voters polled felt the economy was in "good" shape, and that 87% of such voters voted for Bush.

NATIONAL ECONOMY		BUSH	KERRY
TOTAL	2004	2000	2004
Excellent (4%)	89%	+63	11%
Good (43%)	87%	+35	13%
Not Good (35%)	26%	-36	72%
Poor (17%)	6%	-52	92%

27. Find your own example of a similar large group that was heavily pro-Bush and think of some reasons as to why this group might have been so supportive of Bush. You have just performed a bit of political scholarship, dissecting and explaining election results.

28. Repeat steps 26 and 27 for Kerry, the Democratic candidate. Except this time, find a group that is a relatively *small* portion of the electorate (under 25%) and that voted heavily for the Democrat. Think over why this group might have been so supportive of the Democratic candidate. You have just discovered a segment of the electorate that might be interpreted as delivering a clear message to Democratic candidates—but analysts have to be careful in concluding that such a group is delivering a "mandate" for change, since it is so small.

29. Now you are ready to view the 2008 exit polling data. Go to the CNN election center at **www.cnn.com/ELECTION/2008/**. There should be a prominent link for viewing 2008 exit polling data. Click it. If you do not see such a link, type "exit poll 2008" into the search box on this page, and you should be taken to CNN's exit polling data page.

30. Repeat the kinds of analysis you performed in steps 23–28 and explore the 2008 data. Be on the lookout for a voter group that is fairly large in size and that lined up heavily behind the winning presidential candidate. *List this voter group, its percent of the electorate, and the percent that voted for the winning candidate on the worksheet.*

31. Think about why this group might have voted as it did, and what kind of national mood or movement the group may represent. *Use the worksheet to share your brief assessment of whether or not his group was delivering a clear "mandate" for change to the winning candidate.*

32. Based on what you find there, you can elaborate on the motivating issues of a key voter group in the 2008 election. You might find additional data on the group you identified in step 30, or you might discover an entirely new group that can be called vital to this election.

33. For an election to be called a mandate, there should also be clear policy signals from voters. Politicians must be able to tell the message voters were sending, and what policies they want adopted. To determine whether there were any clear policy or issue messages in the election, one strategy is to review opinion polls. Go to **www.pollingreport.com.**

34. You can see a list of polls in a variety of categories, including a "national priorities" poll under the State of the Union Category, and many other relevant polls in the "In the News" and "Issues" categories. Explore a few of these polls, and determine if you can detect a clear mood of the voters in favor of presidential leadership on an issue. *Based on what you find, summarize on the worksheet whether you think there is a clear issue mandate following this election, or not. If you want additional data before you draw your conclusions, you can find it in steps 35 and 36. After following steps 35 and 36, fill in your worksheet as instructed in this step.*

35. Though it is not required to complete this exercise, for additional data, you can explore the wide variety of other political polling websites with good public opinion data. Remember that your task is not just to discover the percent of people supporting one or the other presidential candidate. Rather, you are looking to discover a *unique group of the electorate* (e.g., church-going evangelicals or young Latinos) that seemed to breaking heavily toward the winning candidate, and/or that is clearly voicing a unique concern about public policy (for example, you might find that young voters voted at their highest level ever, and that 80% of them voted largely on the Iraq War issue—you could say that this group was delivering a "mandate" for change on the Iraq War.

36. Here are some good public opinion/polling data websites. There are many other good sites available, and this list is simply suggestive. Visit a few sites, and you will find the kind of data you need.

   - *New York Times* Pollwatch:
     www.nytimes.com/ref/us/polls_index.html
   - *Washington Post* polls: www.washingtonpost.com/wp-dyn/content/politics/polls/index.html
   - CBS news polls:
     www.cbsnews.com/sections/opinion/polls/main500160.shtml

- Long time polling leader—explore the articles and polls in the "Politics" section: www.gallup.com/
- Rasmussen Report polls: www.rasmussenreports.com/public_content/politics

37. Finally, a key part of any presidential mandate is the general perception among the public, the politicians and the pundits that a mandate exists. If people *think* the president has a mandate, they will generally support his leadership and policies, whether or not the voters truly meant to support those ideas in the election. Your final task, therefore, is to examine the "conventional wisdom" around whether the winner of the 2008 election received a popular mandate.

38. To broaden your sense of what the community in general is saying about the idea of a presidential mandate, conduct a Google search of key terms such as: *election, 2008, mandate*. You can also add the name of the election winner to this list. A long list of links will appear.

39. Browse through some of these links, to see if you can detect a general mood of people celebrating and proclaiming the presidential mandate, or vigorously denying that it exists. Pick one or two interesting links to follow and read or view a bit of what you find on this subject.

40. *On the worksheet, summarize what you have discovered through this limited sample of "conventional wisdom" regarding the presidential mandate. Does the conventional wisdom hold that the president received a mandate or not?*

41. You have examined the same kind of data that scholars, politicians, journalists and pundits use to determine whether the voters were delivering a mandate: the size of the president's victory, the number of seats the president's party gained in Congress, the voter groups and policy issues that were important, and the conventional wisdom. *Based on all that data, do you conclude that the president has a mandate for change? Or not? Defend your answer on the worksheet.*

Done!

WAS THERE A MANDATE? WORKSHEET

1. Fill in the missing 2008 election data in the chart below. See steps 10 and 11 for how to calculate the missing data

	Normal Elections	Mandate Elections	Election 2008
Popular Vote Advantage	5.4%	16.6%	
Percent of Electoral Votes	66%	94%	

2. Based on this data, was 2008 a "mandate" election?

3. Fill in the missing 2008 election data in the chart below.

	Normal Elections	Mandate Elections	Election 2008
Seats Gained in the House of Reps. by President's Party	8	39	

4. Based on this data, was 2008 a "mandate" election?

5. Based on 2008 exit polls, Fill in the information below.

Name of Large Voting Group	Percent of the Electorate	Percent Supporting Election Winner

6. Do you think that the voting group in step 5 was delivering a mandate/message to the winning candidate? Why or why not?

7. Based on your review of polling data, did the voters send a policy message that could be considered a mandate? Defend your answer.

8. What did you learn about "conventional wisdom" regarding the existence of a 2008 presidential mandate in your internet search?

9. Considering all the data you found in this exercise, do you conclude that the recently elected president has a mandate? Defend your answer.

ISSUE THREE:
ANALYZING THE PRESIDENTIAL INAUGURAL ADDRESS

It is among the rarest of American political speeches—the presidential inaugural address, which occurs only once every four years. Delivered by each newly elected president since George Washington, the presidential inaugural has grown into what former presidential speechwriter Ted Widmer calls a "Secular Sermon": a speech full of ritual and philosophy in which the most powerful men in the world have shared "their fears, their hopes, and their most personal aspirations for their country."[1] The president will fill the inaugural address with lofty rhetoric, energetic proposals and educational stories, much of the country will watch it, and the address will set the tone for the First 100 Days of the new presidential administration. It is probably the most important speech the new president will give this year, which is saying a good deal since speech-making is one of the most important roles and powers of the president. In a system of democratic checks and balances, such as that of one United States, the president cannot rely on a supportive Congress or military authority to get his or her way—instead, the president must often lead by convincing people with the force of well-expressed ideas. "The power of the presidency is the power to persuade," argued notable presidential scholar Richard Neustadt.[2] A good example of this power of persuasion during the president's "First 100 Days" will be the inaugural address of 2009—delivered on the first day of the First 100 Days.

This exercise will help you to view, analyze and evaluate this year's inaugural address. To help you begin, it is important to have a sense of what is expected of a good inaugural address. Though each inaugural

---

[1] Ted Widmer, "So Help Me God: What all 54 Inaugural Addresses, Taken as One Long Book, Tell Us About American History," *American Scholar*, 74.1(2005): 29–41.
[2] Richard Neudstadt, *Presidential Power and the Modern Presidents*. New York: The Free Press, 1991.

address is unique, each should meet enduring standards in order to be considered great or at least effective. Those standards include:

- Proper use of obligatory rhetoric
- Meeting the expectations and mood of the public
- Addressing current national challenges by setting policy direction for the upcoming "First 100 Days"
- Expressing an underlying philosophy of government and the good society.

Obligatory Rhetoric. Former Clinton speechwriter Ted Widmer argues that a significant amount of every presidential inaugural is made up of "obligatory rhetoric." Americans expect presidents to repeat time-honored rituals in their inaugurals—by doing so, the president shares his understanding of the thread of history uniting the nation, demonstrates that he shares American values, and reassures Americans that the national mission will continue without upheaval, even in this time of transition. "Obligatory" uses of rhetoric include references to national unity after a divisive election; references to American greatness and exceptionalism in the world; appeals to the guidance of God; expressions of faith in democracy, the constitution and the American people; and expressions of thanks and admiration for previous presidents. With tongue in cheek, Widmer describes obligatory rhetoric as a act of "Kabuki" theater, in which the audience derives much of their pleasure from knowing exactly how the play is going to go. As Widmer explains, "the kabuki of the typical inaugural can be broken down into specific set pieces; the thoughts arranged in a comforting ten-step sequence that [is] instantly familiar."

1. I am not worthy of this great honor.
2. But I congratulate the people that they elected me.
3. Now we must all come together, even those of us who really hate each other.
4. I love the Constitution, the Union, and George Washington.
5. I will work against bad threats.
6. I will work for good things.
7. We must avoid entangling alliances.

8. America's strength = democracy.
9. Democracy's strength = America.
10. Thanks, God.[3]

It can be expected that the 2009 inaugural address will include such obligatory "set pieces." If it is a great address, the president will find an innovative way to make these enduring values seem fresh and newly energetic, rising above cliché and allowing the public to glimpse the president's personal connection with enduring national themes.

Public Mood and Expectations. A great presidential speech must also respond to the current mood and expectations of the public. President Reagan's first inaugural in 1981 came after several years of deep American crises (e.g., double-digit inflation and unemployment, the hostage crisis in Iran) that led the previous president (Carter) to conclude that Americans were suffering from a deep depression and "malaise" in the late 1970s. The public mood was depressed and anxious, but hopeful that the new president (Reagan) would bring confidence and strength back to the nation. In his inaugural, President Reagan promised to do just that, speaking with energy about how the "American mission" would be renewed under his leadership and sharing inspiring stories about soldiers who had braved hard ordeals in order to insure that Americans could always live with hope and confidence. Presidential scholars remember Reagan's speech as well suited to the mood and expectations of his time. In 2009, what kind of public mood and expectations will the new president face, and will his inaugural address rise to the occasion?

Set Policy Goals. Presidents must use the inaugural address to set policy goals for the first year of their new administration. Every president faces policy challenges (e.g., health care problems, the global warming challenge, ongoing problems in the Middle East), and the inaugural address is a chance to announce important policy directions in dealing with these challenges. For example, President Franklin Roosevelt's first inaugural announced an ambitious set of policy responses to the Great

---

[3] Ted Widmer, Ibid.

Depression (including public works, agricultural assistance, and banking reform) that quickly were enacted into law during a burst of legislation that became the inspiration behind the notion of the "First 100 Days." To this day, we expect a president to announce a vigorous policy agenda in the inaugural, and we still analyze how well the president did in subsequently leading the nation during his "First 100 Days."

Philosophy of Government and the Good Society. In the best inaugural addresses, presidents are not simply politicians, announcing new policy directions. As the most important source of unity and energy in the American government, presidents must also be philosophers, storytellers and fabulists. In their speeches they must build a philosophy of how government should work, share a convincing vision of the good society, and lead their people toward this philosophy and vision. President Reagan is remembered for his effectiveness in leading the nation toward his inaugural vision that "in this present crisis, government is not the solution to our problem; government is the problem." President Lincoln's poetic testimony to the meaning of the sacrifices of the Civil War elevated his second inaugural to the level of spiritual meditation. In the 2009 inaugural, we can expect again to see the president express an underlying philosophy of what government can and cannot do for its people, and to offer a guiding theory of what makes for a good community.

In this exercise, you will explore the elements that make up an effective inaugural address. You will begin by completing steps 1–9 BEFORE viewing the inaugural address of 2009. Then you will watch the presidential inaugural and explore some of the media coverage following that address. Then you will complete steps 10–14 AFTER viewing the inaugural address. When done, you will be able to offer an assessment of whether the 2009 inaugural address fits into the pantheon of truly great American moments.

ANALYZING THE PRESIDENTIAL INAUGURAL ADDRESS

Complete steps 1–9 BEFORE viewing the presidential inaugural; Complete steps 10–16 AFTER viewing the inaugural

1. A good way to gain perspective on whether this year's inaugural address will be remembered as a landmark event, an average address, or a failed speech is to examine previous inaugurals widely regarded as successes and failures.

2. To begin, go to **www.presidentialrhetoric.com**. This website has an archive of all presidential inaugural addresses through history (available by clicking on the **"Historical Speech Archive"** link on the right hand side of the page). Even better, you can *listen* to many of these speeches over your computer by clicking on the link for **"Top 100 Speeches of the Twentieth Century."**

3. Three presidential inaugural addresses widely regarded as great successes were the first inaugurals of Presidents Franklin D. Roosevelt and John F. Kennedy, and the second inaugural address of President

Lincoln. To listen to Roosevelt's and Kennedy's speech, click the link to the **"Top 100 Speeches of the Twentieth Century"** (the link with the picture of President Franklin Roosevelt to the right hand side of the website).

4. The following screen appears, allowing you to peruse the list of the top 100 speeches of the 1900s, according to the scholars at presidentialrhetoric.com. Click the "mp3" option under the audio column to listen to the inaugural speeches of President Kennedy and President Franklin Roosevelt (rated as the 2nd and 3rd greatest speeches, respectively).

As you listen to the speeches, it will be useful to know that President Roosevelt's address was delivered just as a Democratic president replaced a Republican in the midst of the Great Depression. Americans were fearful for their future. President Kennedy's speech was delivered at the dawn of the 1960s, when American affluence and confidence were soaring after winning World War II and experiencing a dramatic burst of technological and economic growth.

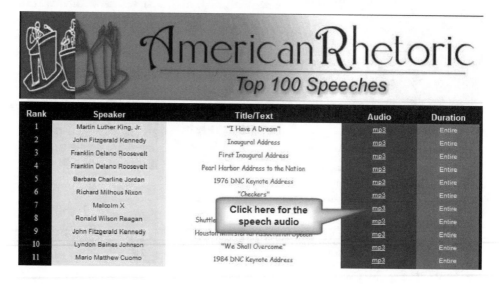

American Rhetoric
Top 100 Speeches

Rank	Speaker	Title/Text	Audio	Duration
1	Martin Luther King, Jr.	"I Have A Dream"	mp3	Entire
2	John Fitzgerald Kennedy	Inaugural Address	mp3	Entire
3	Franklin Delano Roosevelt	First Inaugural Address	mp3	Entire
4	Franklin Delano Roosevelt	Pearl Harbor Address to the Nation	mp3	Entire
5	Barbara Charline Jordan	1976 DNC Keynote Address	mp3	Entire
6	Richard Milhous Nixon	"Checkers"	mp3	Entire
7	Malcolm X		mp3	Entire
8	Ronald Wilson Reagan	Shuttle	mp3	Entire
9	John Fitzgerald Kennedy	Houston	mp3	Entire
10	Lyndon Baines Johnson	"We Shall Overcome"	mp3	Entire
11	Mario Matthew Cuomo	1984 DNC Keynote Address	mp3	Entire

Click here for the speech audio

5. If you have problems listening to the audio, you can access the text of the speeches under the "Title/Text" column on this same page.

6. The text (but not audio) of earlier presidential inaugurals can be found by returning to the homepage of presidentialrhetoric.com and clicking the **"Historical Speech Archive"** link to the right of your page (the link with the picture of President Jefferson).

7. When the following screen appears, click the links to President Lincoln's second inaugural and President McKinley's first inaugural. Read the text of the speeches that appear. President Lincoln's is very short and is remembered as a great success, while McKinley's is lengthy and is remembered as a very poor inaugural address. You may skim McKinley's speech, just to get a sense of his policy focus and the style of his rhetoric. As you read the speeches, it will be useful to know that President Lincoln's address was delivered in the midst of the horribly divisive civil war, and McKinley's was delivered in the midst of the industrial revolution, as the country struggled with questions such as government deficits, immigration, and tariffs.

Abraham Lincoln	First Inaugural Address Second Inaugural Address	1861 | 1862 | 1863 | 1864
Andrew Johnson		
Ulysses Grant	First Inaugural Address Second Inaugural Address	Click the links for Lincoln's second Inaugural and McKinley's first Inaugural
Rutherford Hayes	Inaugural Address	
James Garfield	Inaugural Address	
Chester Arthur		
Grover Cleveland	First Inaugural Address	
Benjamin Harrison	Inaugural Address	
Grover Cleveland	Second Inaugural Address	
William McKinley	First Inaugural Address Second Inaugural Address	

8. Having listened to the inaugural addresses of Presidents Kennedy and Franklin Roosevelt, and having read the inaugural addresses of President Lincoln and President McKinley, why do you think Lincoln's, Roosevelt's and Kennedy's addresses are widely regarded as landmark successes, while McKinley's address is remembered as a dismal failure? Summarize some of the strong points of Lincoln, Roosevelt and/or Kennedy's speech and also summarize your thoughts on the weaknesses of McKinley's address. *Fill in the worksheet.*

9. To be successful, a president's inaugural must use powerful rhetoric. But it must also accurately respond to the mood and needs of the country at the time. How would you describe the national mood and public expectations as the nation awaits the 2009 presidential inaugural address? What is the public feeling and what are the most pressing challenges that the nation expects the new president to address? In your response, you should reference at least one outside source (e.g., news editorial or journal article) that has been influential in your thinking. *Fill in the worksheet.*

10. You will fill in the rest of the worksheet AFTER viewing the 2009 Presidential Inaugural Address. As you watch that address, you should be attuned to the "enduring standards" that all inaugural addresses are expected to meet. As discussed in the overview to this exercise, those standards are:

   - Proper use of obligatory rhetoric
   - Ability to meet the expectations and mood of the public
   - Ability to address current national challenges by setting policy direction for the upcoming "First 100 Days"
   - Ability to express an underlying philosophy of government and the good society.

11. After you have viewed the address, this exercise will ask you to comment on how well the 2009 inaugural address met those enduring standards. To prepare for your inaugural address viewing, therefore, you should read over the next steps, so that you know what you will be

looking for in the address. After the speech is over, proceed with the following steps and fill in the remainder of the worksheet.

12. Having viewed the 2009 inaugural address, how do you rate the president's use of "obligatory rhetoric"? (See exercise overview for more detail on "obligatory rhetoric.")

Fill in the worksheet by rating the president on this category as either:

- **Poor** (very few references to obligatory themes such as American greatness, the guidance of God, or thanking previous presidential leaders; or the references that are offered are uninspired, dull, predictable and forgettable)

- **Average** (adequate references to obligatory themes, and references are adequately interesting and memorable)

- **Good** (references to obligatory themes are offered in a creative and memorable way that leaves the listener inspired about the nation, the moment, or the president himself)

Provide one example of obligatory rhetoric (or the lack thereof) in the president's speech that support your assessment.

13. How well did the president's speech respond to the national mood, public expectations and/or current challenges that you laid out in your answer to step 9 of this exercise?

Fill in the worksheet by rating the president on this category as either:

- **Poor** (Address seemed unconnected to the current public mood; president is out of touch with important expectations of the public)

- **Average** (President adequately connected to public mood and expectations; address was well received)

- **Good** (President perfectly captured spirit and mood of the day; innovative speech infused the public with confidence and inspired high expectations)

Provide one example of the how the president attempted to describe and connect to the public mood.

14. Having viewed the inaugural address, how do you rate the president's proposal of new policy directions as a response to the challenges of the time?

Fill in the worksheet by rating the president on this category as either:

- **Poor** (Policy discussion in the speech was either incoherent and not targeted at the challenges of the moment, or the president provided either excessive or inadequate detail on his/her policy ideas, thus turning off much of the audience)

- **Average** (The president recognized the important challenges of the day and offered credible policy solutions, with appropriate level of detail)

- **Good** (The president laid out a clear and persuasive action agenda that drew from his/her underlying theory of government and that provided a persuasive sense of direction and energy in the new presidency)

Provide an example of policy direction that is laid out in the president's speech and that supports your assessment.

15. Having viewed the inaugural address, how do you rate the president's ability to express an underlying theory of government and/or the good society in his address?

Fill in the worksheet by rating the president on this category as either:

- **Poor** (Inadequate or uninspired attention to underlying philosophy of government and society, or muddled and incoherent in his/her overall vision)

- **Average** (Adequate references to the president's underlying philosophy of government and society. Philosophy offered in a way that gives listener confidence that the president has an underlying direction and coherent set of values)

- **Good** (President's overall vision of government and the good society offered in such an innovative and inspirational way that listeners are likely to be persuaded in favor of the president's vision; the President was successful in educating the nation in his way of thinking)

Provide an example of philosophical thinking/rhetoric in the president's speech that supports your assessment.

16. Overall, how do you rate the president's inaugural address? Will it be remembered as a stunning success, a dismal failure, or as an adequate/average address? *Summarize your assessment on the worksheet, drawing on the knowledge you have built in this exercise.*

To assist in your evaluation, read at least two outside news/journal articles that provide timely commentary on the speech. Good sources are the *New York Times* (**www.nyt.com**), the *National Review* (**www.nationalreview.com**; a leading journal of conservative thought) or the *American Prospect* (**www.prospect.org**; a leading journal of liberal thought).

Done!

ANALYZING THE INAUGURAL ADDRESS WORKSHEET

1. Why are Lincoln's, Roosevelt's, and/or Kennedy's inaugurals seen as successes, while McKinley's is remembered as a failure?

2. What is the public mood and expectation as the nation awaits the Inaugural? What fears and/or hopes does the president need to address, and what policy challenges are people seeking leadership on?

3. Rate the president's use of obligatory rhetoric.

Rating	Example to Support Assessment

4. Rate how well the president responded to the national mood.

Rating	Example to Support Assessment

5. Rate how well the president laid out persuasive policy proposals.

Rating	Example to Support Assessment

6. Rate how well the president expressed a vision of the good society.

Rating	Example to Support Assessment

7. Provide an overall assessment of the president's Inaugural. Cite at least two outside sources that have informed your assessment.

ISSUE FOUR: ALL THE PRESIDENT'S MEN
LESSONS OF THE PRESIDENTIAL CABINET

From the very beginning of the presidency, presidents have surrounded themselves with a cabinet—top-level advisors and administrators who together say a good deal about the priorities and political motivations of the nation's chief executive. The Constitution gives the authority for such presidential advisors in Article II, section 2, which states that:

> *The President . . . may require the opinion, in writing, of the principal Officer in each of the executive Departments, upon any subject relating to the Duties of their respective Offices. And He shall have Power to appoint . . . by and with the Advice and Consent of the Senate, all other Officers of the United States . . . which shall be established by Law.*

Cabinet members are the secretaries of executive departments that have been established by Congress over the years, namely the secretaries of Agriculture, Commerce, Defense, Education, Energy, Health and Human Services, Homeland Security, Housing and Urban Development, Interior, Labor, State, Transportation, Treasury, Veterans Affairs, and the Attorney General. It is natural to think that a freshly elected president would fill these vital positions with the "best person for the job." But of course, it's not as easy as that. For example, just what is the "job" of a cabinet secretary? Managing the department, to be sure—and most nominees are capable of doing that. But beyond running the department capably—what do presidents expect of their cabinet secretaries?

Presidents actually have various political calculations that shape who they choose as cabinet officials.[1] For example, presidents have to be careful that their new cabinet "looks like America," in Bill Clinton's terms. A cabinet made up only of elderly, white male millionaires wouldn't be well received today. A president also needs nominees who reward his political

---

[1] See, for example, MaryAnne Borelli, *The President's Cabinet.* Boulder, CO: Lynne Rienner, 2002.

supporters, and who build relationships with political groups that he needs to work with while governing. A president needs to send symbolic messages to the country about his commitment to such things as civil rights and national defense, and a president wants nominees who share his ideology and are committed to moving the president's agenda and policy priorities.

It is important that a new president assembles a cabinet that meets these various priorities. In this exercise, you will learn about the calculations presidents make in assembling their cabinet, and will draw conclusions about the message that the new president is sending with the cabinet he is building. Is the cabinet a group of ideologues, committed to moving an agenda? Or did the president build a cabinet around political payback, bridge-building with opposed political groups, or making sure his team reflected America's demographics? What will your research reveal?

LESSONS OF THE PRESIDENTIAL CABINET

1. You will begin your study of the meaning of the new presidential cabinet by reviewing a bit of the historic role of this group of presidential advisors.

2. As you learned in the overview to this lesson, the Cabinet is a group of presidential advisors who have important authority to shape rules and priorities in specific public policy areas (e.g., the secretary of the Department of Justice administers and enforces the nation's laws, while the Labor secretary enforces rules specific to labor issues and attends to the health of the nation's workforce). You can see a general overview of the role of the overall cabinet by going to **http://www.whitehouse.gov/government/cabinet.html** (screenshot below is from the George W. Bush White House).

3. Learn more about the history and role of the presidential cabinet by going to **http://usgovinfo.about.com/blcababout.htm.** Review the details you find there.

4. *Based on what you have learned at these websites, fill in your worksheet with the answers to Question 1: Who appoints and who "consents" or confirms nominees to U.S. cabinet positions?*

5. As described on usgovinfo.about.com, "the word 'Cabinet' comes from the Italian word 'Cabinetto,' meaning a 'small, private room': a good place to discuss important business without being interrupted." You can see the actual "small, private room" where the president meets his Cabinet at **www.whitehouse.gov/government/cabinet-room.html**. There are also some interesting details about who sits where in the Cabinet room, and why.

6. You have reviewed some of the basics of the role of the president's cabinet. Now you can begin analyzing the details of the incoming president's cabinet, and begin to draw scholarly conclusions about what kind of cabinet the president is constructing. What political debts is the president paying off with his new cabinet, what new groups is he reaching out to, what message is he trying to send, and what policy agenda is he preparing to move? You can determine many of these things by looking at how the president's first cabinet unfolds.

7. As discussed in the overview to this lesson, presidents ponder various different political calculations in deciding who to appoint to their cabinet. Various lists of calculations might be constructed by different scholars, but for this lab you will consider the following calculations that presidents make as they construct their cabinet (the list is taken loosely from the previously cited analysis in MaryAnne Borelli's book, *The President's Cabinet*).

- **Substantive Agenda:** Presidents appoint cabinet officials who will help the president advance a specific ideology and agenda; for example, a president might appoint someone to fulfill the attorney general's position who shares his priority to prosecute corporate crime.

- **Descriptive Representation:** Presidents appoint cabinet officials who can represent "what America looks like," in the phrasing of President Bill Clinton. Presidents often want a cabinet to have a diverse mix of women, men, different races and ethnicities, and people from various geographical areas of the country.

- **Indebtedness:** Presidents appoint cabinet officials to meet political debts. That is, they might appoint Cabinet members who are beloved by certain interest groups, political leaders, or voter groups who were important in helping the president to win the election.

- **Political Relationships:** Presidents appoint cabinet officials to build relationships with important political groups. For example, a president might appoint an official who is expected to work with Congress, or who is well-respected in the American South, or who comes from the oil and gas industry.

- **Symbolism:** Presidents appoint cabinet officials who can convey important symbolic messages. Those messages might relate to conveying the patriotism and strength of the president himself (by appointing a patriotic war hero, for example), or to conveying the president's approach to a specific issue (such as appointing several pro-labor cabinet officials, or appointing a group of "hawks" to foreign policy positions).

Of course, a single cabinet appointment can and often does fulfill several of these various roles. But in general, different cabinet officials seem to fit more in one kind of role than another, and scholars and pundits make a living by reading the tea leaves of what the president is "saying" with his first cabinet appointments.

You can read the tea leaves, too! In the next steps, you will review the appointees of the new president, and draw conclusions about what roles these appointees are filling and what messages they are sending.

8. You can begin by reviewing the way in which the new president is seeking "descriptive" diversity in his cabinet by building a group that "looks like America." When scholars speak of "descriptive" diversity, they usually are talking about the extent to which a group includes

members from groups that have often been *underrepresented* in American history (such as women, blacks, Latinos, other race/ethnic groups, the gay and lesbian community, etc.). "Descriptive" representation might also mean including members from different geographical areas of the country (e.g., the South, or the Rocky Mountain West), from different age groups, and the like.

9. How did past presidents do in meeting the goal of descriptive diversity? Here is some interesting data about the gender and racial diversity of the initial Cabinet of all presidents since Lyndon Johnson (1965–1968).

- Lyndon Johnson (1965–1968): All white men

- Richard Nixon (1969–1974): All white men

- Gerald Ford (1974–1976): All white men

- Jimmy Carter (1977–1980): 2 white women, 13 white men

- Ronald Reagan (1981–1988): 1 black man, 1 white woman, 13 white men

- George H.W. Bush (1989–1992): 2 Hispanics, 1 black, 2 women, 9 white men

- Bill Clinton (1993–2000): 4 women, 4 blacks, 2 Hispanics, 9 whites, 10 men (categories overlap).

- George W. Bush (2001–2008): 3 women, 2 Hispanics, 2 blacks, 2 Asians, 9 whites and 12 men (categories overlap).

10. In terms of securing "descriptive" representation of different races, ethnicities and sexes on the cabinet, what has been the trend between 1965 and 2008? Has the cabinet become more diverse, less diverse, generally stayed the same, achieved perfect diversity, or what? *Indicate the answer on the worksheet.*

11. Now you can evaluate how the new president's cabinet fits into this general trend. You can view the members of the president's new cabinet by going to **www.whitehouse.gov/government/cabinet.html**

(see previous screenshot in this lab). You can review photos of the members, and learn more about their background by clicking the links near the photos.

12. Begin by filling in the names of the new cabinet officials (and their offices) on the attached worksheets, titled: "Building the Cabinet: Presidential Political Calculations," and "Reviewing the Cabinet: Assessing Ideology."

13. *Based on this review, you can fill in the first column of the attached worksheet, titled "Building the Cabinet: Presidential Political Calculations."* The column is titled "Descriptive Representation." Under this column, fill in the appropriate demographic characteristics of each member of the new cabinet. For example, add a short phrase such as "black man," "white man," "Hispanic woman," "gay man," or whatever the case may be. When you are done, you can make some assessment about the level of "descriptive representation" in the president's new cabinet. At the end of this lab, you will be able to share some of your general assessment on this point, and/or on others.

If you cannot determine all the data you need from the whitehouse.gov website, conduct a Google search with such terms as "president," "cabinet," "nominees" and "diversity." You should find several articles providing the information you need to fill in the chart.

14. Your "Presidential Political Calculations" has several other columns. Your next step is to determine, for each cabinet member, whether that member was appointed to fulfill the president's goals of moving a "substantive agenda," to cover his "political indebtedness," to pursue "political relationship building," or to send an important "symbolic message." As you draw conclusions, you can fill in each box with a short word or phrase describing your findings. Some boxes will be empty (or N/A), if the cabinet official does not match the goals of that category. Other times, several boxes for a secretary will be filled in with information, since there are often various political roles reasons why a president would appoint any given secretary.

See below for an example of how your data will look, when filled in completely for a hypothetical cabinet member. In this example, John

Doe is a white career military officer, with a record of being a strong "hawk" on how the United States should approach the Middle East. Appointing John Doe as secretary of Defense is seen as helping the new president build a relationship with the military community and to send a message that his administration will be vigorous in confronting threats in the Middle East. John Doe was NOT appointed to move forward a specific agenda of the president, nor to fulfill a political debt, since the military community was not an ally of the president during the election (in this example).

Cabinet Member	Descriptive Representation	Substantive Agenda	Political Debt	Relationship Building	Symbolic Message
John Doe, Sec. of Defense	White Man	N/A	N/A	Career Military	Strong on Terrorism

15. Where will you find the information you need to fill out your worksheet? You can begin by revisiting a site you have seen earlier in this lab. Go to **www.whitehouse.gov/government/cabinet.html** and you will find detail on each of the new cabinet members. As you review this site, and the sites in the following steps (16–21), be sure that you take notes so that you can accurately fill in the worksheet titled "Presidential Political Calculations" with information for each of the Cabinet officials.

16. An encyclopedic site that provide an overview of the background of various Cabinet appointees is **www.votesmart.org**.

On this site, as seen in the screenshot below, you should go to the dropdown menu under "Officials," and click on "Presidents and Executive Branch." A "Presidents and Executive Branch" page will load, with links for each of the new cabinet members. Click on any link to learn more about any of these officials.

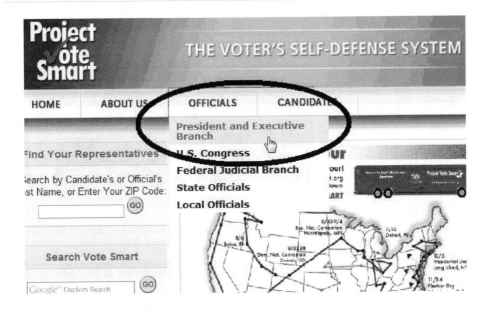

17. Finally, you can review what the journalists and pundits are saying about the new cabinet. Conduct a simple Google search for news articles with terms such as "presidential," "cabinet," "appointment," and "politics," and you should find some articles analyzing the political calculations behind the new appointees.

18. Alternatively, you can view televised journalism on this subject. Go to **http://www.cnn.com/video/.** You are now at the video archive section of CNN news.

19. Toward the bottom of the page, you can search videos by category. Scroll down to the bottom of the page and click the button to search videos **"By Section"** (see screenshot).

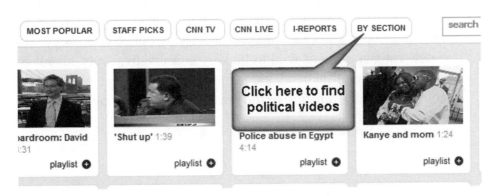

20. A menu of CNN video sections appears to the left of the video thumbnails. Click on the **"Politics"** section, as in the screenshot below.

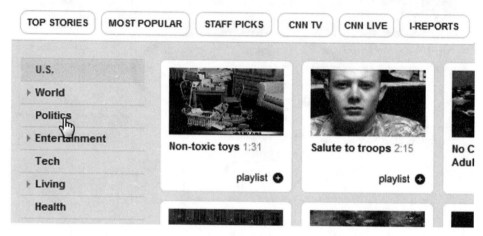

21. Thumbnails of the political videos appear, together with short titles. Browse through the video clips and choose one or two that seem to be focused on the cabinet selection process. If possible, find a video on the political calculations that are influencing the construction of the cabinet. Watch that video or videos.

22. *Now that you have reviewed a variety of data sources, you can finish filling in the worksheet, "Building a Cabinet: Presidential Political Calculations."* Not every box will be filled in for every new cabinet official. Follow the guidance of the sample worksheet following step 14.

23. Once done, you are now ready to fill out a different worksheet, with a different kind of assessment of new cabinet members. Cabinet appointees fulfill important roles such as sending symbolic messages and building new political relations—but another way to examine cabinet members is to examine their underlying political ideology. Do the new cabinet officials tend to be very conservative, very liberal or generally middle-of-the-road and mainstream? What general direction, ideologically, does it look like the president will be taking America in his first year?

24. To address this question, you will fill in the worksheet: "Reviewing the New Cabinet: Assessing Political Ideology." This worksheet has a space for all new cabinet members. *Fill in each slot with the name of a cabinet member.*

25. For each new cabinet member, you can now check a box in the "Ideology Scale" that is provided to the right of each name. You will be offering your own assessments of where secretaries fit ideologically. Because "ideology" is a "loose" term, without perfect definitions, your assessment might vary from other people's assessment. It is not so vital that you place each member in the "right" space—rather it is important that you have clear reasons for why you choose the category that you do—and that you can explain those reasons to your professor if asked.

26. For the following steps, you will assess where each new member best fits. Is the new secretary:

- **Strongly Conservative?** (Defined by such things as emphasizing his/her support of the business world, advocating the role of personal responsibility in achieving success, advocating for strong military and police forces to secure order and safety, and advocating for a significant role for church, faith and "family values" in public life.)

- **Extremely Liberal?** (Defined by such things as emphasizing the need for government to address social problems like race, poverty, and gender inequality, emphasizing the role of non-profits, social movements and government regulation to improve society, and emphasizing the need to pursue social justice by limiting the ability of the powerful to harm the "little guy"?

- **Mainstream/Middle of the Road?** (Defined by a secretary who seems neither extremely conservative nor extremely liberal—but who seems moderate and pragmatic, occupying a space at the center of American politics).

27. *Fill in the "Ideology Rankings" worksheet by checking an ideology box for each of the new cabinet officials.* To guide you in your choices, remember what you learned in steps 16–20. When you are done, you can review your meter to determine if the new president is constructing a liberal cabinet far to the "left" of the American mainstream, a conservative cabinet that is far to the "right," or one that is more in the middle.

28. You are now done with gathering data and are ready to offer your final conclusions about the message that the president's new cabinet delivers. Think carefully about what the most important lesson of all this data is, and fill in your final conclusion(s) on the worksheet (question 3 on the worksheet). You may want to comment on the notion of "descriptive representation" and how it relates to the new cabinet. Or perhaps you have conclusions about the overall policy direction in which the new president seems to be going? Does it look like the new president is sending a symbolic message to Americans? What is it? *Add your open-ended, concluding thoughts to the worksheet (question 3).*

Done!

LESSONS OF THE PRESIDENTIAL CABINET

1. Who appoints and who confirms members of the cabinet?

2. In terms of "descriptive representation," how have cabinets changed since the Eisenhower presidency in the 1950s?

3. What are your conclusions about the president's new cabinet? You may comment on such things as descriptive representation, or on such things as what kind of message the president is conveying with his cabinet (complete this step after filling in the charts that follow).

Building the Cabinet: Presidential Political Calculations

Cabinet Member	Descriptive Representation	Substantive Agenda	Political Debt	Relationship Building	Symbolic Message

Cabinet Member	Descriptive Representation	Substantive Agenda	Political Debt	Relationship Building	Symbolic Message

Reviewing the New Cabinet: Assessing Political Ideology
(As you learn about cabinet secretaries, fill in the chart below)

Place an "X" in the each box that that best describes the ideology of each cabinet secretary

Cabinet Secretaries	Very Liberal	Liberal	Middle/ Moderate	Conser-vative	Very Conser-vative

ISSUE FIVE: GUNS OR BUTTER?
EXAMINING PRESIDENTIAL BUDGET PRIORITIES

In 2008, President Bush submitted a budget calling for $2.9 trillion in spending, the largest in American history. Just eight years earlier, Clinton's federal budget topped out at $1.8 trillion. What budget numbers will the new president propose and where will he propose spending those dollars? Students can learn about presidential priorities and the state of the nation by "following the money" and examining how the president proposes to dispose of about $3 trillion dollars in the coming year.

Though much of the presidential budget simply continues expenditure patterns from previous years (partly because almost half of the budget is "mandatory" spending on such items as Social Security and interest on the debt), there is also substantial room for a president to advance his own political priorities through the budget process. About half of the budget is "discretionary" spending that presidential leadership can shift in one direction or another. In thinking about how to spend these "discretionary" dollars, the president must make important choices. Should military spending be increased? Do we need more money to support the Labor Department or to expand social programs like Medicare and education? How large should we let the national deficit grow? The president's budget reflects important choices on such questions, making choices between such fundamental priorities as more "guns" (military spending) or more "butter" (social program spending). Or perhaps we can more guns AND more butter, and pay for it all with a growing national deficit?

Each year, the president is required to submit a federal budget to Congress for the upcoming fiscal year. This budget for the upcoming fiscal year (which begins October 1) is generally submitted soon after Congress convenes in January, and the president commonly defends the policy directions and spending priorities encoded in this budget in his state of the union address around the same time. The budget, which defines which federal departments will grow and which will shrink, and which provides funding to some new policy directions while allowing others to wither, reflects the national priorities and economic thinking of the president. For example, during the Reagan presidency (1980s), defense spending grew substantially compared to the previous President Carter years (reflecting Reagan's commitment to a strengthened military), while during the George W. Bush presidency, the national deficit has been allowed to climb to historic levels.[1]

An incoming president usually submits his overall budget priorities soon after taking office in January, and submits his full budget later in the spring. For example, during his first year in office, President George W. Bush did not submit his first full budget proposal until April 2001, two full months later than the deadline for a sitting president.

In this exercise, you will examine the first budget proposal of the newly elected president. You will examine how much of the budget is off-limits to alteration by any specific president, either because it pays for necessary ongoing expenses that a president can't do much to alter (such as military salaries, or national parks' maintenance), or because it pays for "statutory" programs such as Social Security or Medicare that provide government payments to individuals as a matter of law (thus they are called "mandatory" spending). You will also examine the portions of the budget that are susceptible to presidential alteration, and will judge how the new president is continuing or changing policy priorities of the previous president (Bush).

Now that America has a new president for the first time in almost a decade, it will be interesting to see what priorities are revealed in the new president's budget: more "guns," more "butter," or both with more deficits?

---

[1] Bill Heniff, Jr., "The Role of the President in Budget Development" (CRS Report for Congress, 2003). www.rules.house.gov/archives/RS20179.pdf (accessed on October 1, 2008).

EXAMINING THE PRESIDENTIAL BUDGET

1. The internet is packed with resources for examining the federal budget process. Resources include the White House's budget page (**www.whitehouse.gov/omb/budget**), the Congressional Budget Office (**www.cbo.gov**), the Center for Budget Policy and Priorities (**www.cbpp.org**), the Government Printing Office's budget portal (**www.gpoaccess.gov/usbudget**), and the budget research guide of the University of California, Berkeley (**www.lib.berkeley.edu/doemoff/ govinfo/federal/gov_fed_budget.html**), just to name a few. To get a sense of the range of resources available, you might want to explore a few of these sites, especially the UC-Berkeley site, which has a nice, short description of the federal budget process.

2. To help you better understand this year's presidential budget proposal, begin by going to **www.cbo.gov**. On this page, you will see links to recent budget news, budget projections, an analysis of the president's budgetary proposals, and recent publications of the Congressional Budget Office. At the top of the page, you will see a link titled "About CBO." Click it and you will see a drop down menu, which leads you to documents with more information on what the Congressional Budget Office actually does (i.e., the "CBO Fact Sheet," and the "CBO Role in the Budget Process").

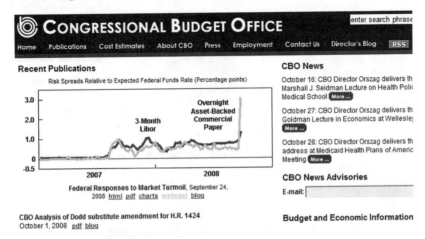

3. The home page of the Congressional Budget Office (www.cbo.gov) includes links to documents organized under sections titled "Recent Publications" and "Frequently Requested." Follow the links and browse one or two documents that look interesting in these sections.

4. *Based on your review in step 3, use the worksheet to briefly summarize one key lesson that you learned from this material.*

5. Go to **www.cbpp.org/pubs/fedbud.htm**. The Center for Budget and Policy Priorities is a non-partisan budget analysis think-tank.

6. On the right hand side of this website are links to various articles and resources about the federal budget process, organized by year (in the section titled "Federal Budget Publications Library"). In the center of the webpage, under the "**Features**" section, are links to a number of useful "introductions" to the federal budget process. In this section, **explore any additional links you like, but *at least* click the link for the slideshow called "Federal Budget Overview" (see screenshot).**

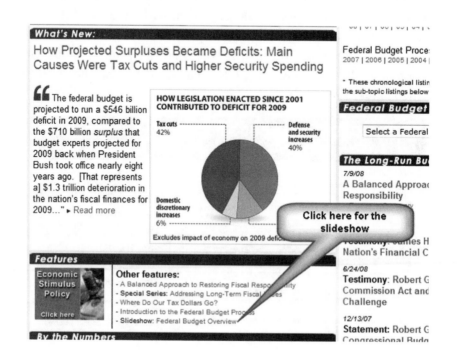

7. Peruse this slide show, pausing at the slides that most interest you and skimming others. Whatever other slides you spend time on, make sure you study slide 4 carefully. *Based on this slide show review, answer the following two questions on your worksheet.*

- *What was the consequence of George W. Bush's budgets between 2001 and 2006, in terms of budget surpluses and deficits (see slide 4)?*

- *What is another interesting budget fact you have learned from any of the other slides?*

8. You have been introduced to basic budget dynamics and to some web resources on the subject. You will now supplement that knowledge with some historical perspective. Go to **www.gpoaccess.gov/usbudget**. This is a web portal to a tremendous range of government budget documents. You will explore just one tiny bit of it.

9. Scroll down the page and highlight the **"FY 2009 Historical Tables"** option in the dropdown menu (see screenshot), and fill in the words **"Table of Contents"** in the Search box, as in the screenshot below. This will take you to a listing of important historical budget tables on this website.

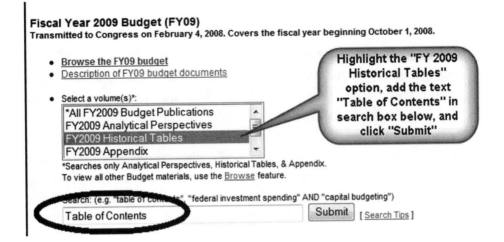

10. You are taken to a page of search results, consisting of a list of federal budget charts. You are interested in finding the chart that will allow you to examine broad historical trends in presidential budgets over the years. To find that kind of chart, scroll down the list of charts until you come to **"Table 4.2: Percentage Distribution of Outlays by Agency: 1962–2012."** This table will be search result 23, or very close to it. Select either the "txt" or "pdf" version of this chart.

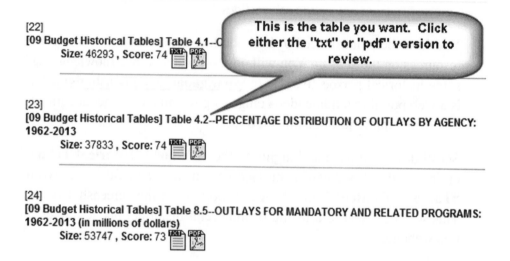

11. You are taken to a table produced by the White House's Office of Management and Budget that allows you to compare federal budgets from 1962 all the way until 2013 (the future budgets are projections/predictions based on current patterns). The table shows what percentage of the budget has gone to various federal departments over the years. For example, in the screenshot below, you can see that the Department of Defense received over 40% of the budget in the 1960s, while Health and Human Services (e.g., welfare and public health spending) accounted for only about 4% of all federal spending.

Table 4.2--PERCENTAGE DISTRIBUTION OF OUTLAYS

Department or other unit	1962	1963	1964
Legislative Branch	0.2	0.2	0.2
The Judiciary	0.1	0.1	0.1
Agriculture	6.0	6.7	6.4
Commerce	0.2	0.3	0.6
Defense--Military	46.9	45.9	44.4
Education	0.8	0.9	0.8
Energy	2.6	2.4	2.3
Health and Human Services	3.3	3.7	3.9
Homeland Security	0.5	0.6	0.6
Housing and Urban Development	0.8	-0.5	0.1
Interior	0.6	0.7	0.6
Justice	0.2	0.2	0.2
Labor	3.7	3.2	2.9
State	0.4	0.5	0.4
Transportation	3.6	3.7	4.0
Treasury	7.9	8.6	8.7
Veterans Affairs	5.2	4.9	4.8

12. Scroll through this chart, and pay attention to what happens to three departments: **Agriculture** (assistance to farmers)**, Defense,** and **Health and Human Services** (social programs such as welfare, Medicare, and housing assistance). Compare how these departments fared between three different sets of presidents, as listed below.

- 1976–1980 (Carter-D) versus 1981–1991 (Reagan-R)

- 1981–1991 (Bush-R) versus 1992–2000 (Clinton-D)

- 1992–2000 (Clinton-D) versus 2001–2008 (Bush-R)

Comparing these sets of years, you should discover some patterns in what tends to happen to Agriculture, Defense and Human Services spending when Republicans (Bush and Reagan) hold the presidency versus what happens under the Democrats (Carter and Clinton). *Based on this review, fill in the worksheet with what you have learned. Make sure you note which area of spending seems most dramatically affected (up or down) based on which party holds the presidency.*

13. For a final bit of historical context, investigate the historical pattern of deficit spending, under Republican versus Democratic presidents. Deficit spending occurs when the government spends more than it receives in the form of tax revenues. The federal government must borrow money from lenders in such situations and pay it back later, with interest. According to the historical pattern, does it matter

whether a Democrat or a Republican holds the presidency, in terms of levels of government debt?

14. To answer that question, go to the Heritage Foundation's "Budget Chart Book" at **www.heritage.org/Research/Features/**. When you get to the website, click the **"Budget Chart Book"** link. The charts in this book are based on official government budget data.

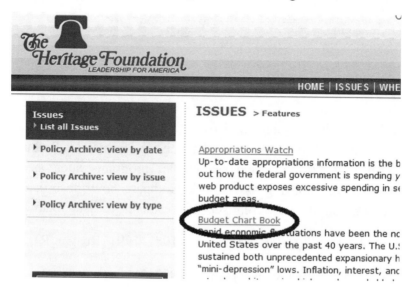

15. You will be taken to the Heritage Foundation's "Federal Revenue and Spending Book of Charts." Click on the **"Contents"** link in the menu bar at the top of the page to see what charts are in the book.

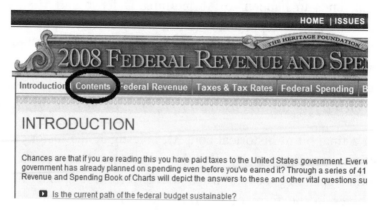

16. You are taken to a list of charts in the book. Scroll down to Section IV, "Revenue and Spending Comparisons." To compare the size of budget

deficits in different presidencies, click on the chart titled "**All Recent Administrations Ran Up Budget Deficits,**" in Section IV.

> ▶ Retired Workers Receive the Largest Share of Social Security Benefits
>
> **IV. REVENUE AND SPENDING COMPARISONS**
>
> ▶ Federal Spending Is Growing Faster Than Federal Revenue
> ▶ Government Spending Grew Faster Than Revenues for Most Administrations
> ▶ All Recent Administrations Ran Up Budget Deficits
> ▶ Among Recent Administrations, President Reagan Stands Out as Most Willing to Use Veto
> ▶ FY 2008 Had the Second-Highest Number of Earmarks in History Despite the Change in Congress
> ▶ Defense Spending Is on the Decline Despite the War on Terrorism
> ▶ Non-Defense Spending Growth Was Lowest Under the Reagan Administration
>
> **V. PROJECTED SPENDING**
>
> ▶ Entitlement Spending Will More Than Double by 2050
> ▶ The Ratio of Elderly to Younger People Is Rapidly Increasing
> ▶ Mandatory Spending Consumes Growing Share of Total Spending

This is the chart you should review

17. The chart that appears shows the average size of each president's budget deficit, as a percent of national gross domestic product. Presidents Nixon, Ford, Reagan, Bush and Bush were Republicans, while Presidents Kennedy, Johnson, Carter, and Clinton were Democrats. Analyze the chart and draw conclusions about whether Democrats or Republicans tend to run bigger deficits. *Fill in your answer on the worksheet. Are you surprised with the result? Why or why not?*

18. You now have some foundation for a better understanding of the current president's budget proposal and how it fits into historical context. To begin to analyze the current president's budget proposal, you can review the president's inaugural/state of the union address where budget priorities were laid out to the American people, and compare them to the previous addresses of President George W. Bush. To find an archive of presidential state of the union addresses, go to the archives of the American Presidency Project at **http://www.presidency.ucsb.edu/sou.php**.

19. Scroll down this page and you will find links to the addresses of all American presidents. One at a time, **select the links to the Inaugural Address of the current present**, read the address, and then repeat this

process for the **links to the 2001 and 2007 addresses of George W. Bush**.

President:	Political Time *(see notes in last paragraph above)*					
	years of term	1st	2nd	3rd	4th	end 4th
George W. Bush	2005-pres.	2005	2006	2007	2008	
	2001-2005	2001*	2002	2003	2004	
William J. Clinton	1997-2001	1997	1998	1999	2000	
	1993-	1993*	1994	1995	1996	
Ge	1993	1989*	1990	1991	1992	
Ron	85-1989	1985	1986	1987	1988	
	1981-1985		1982	1983	1984	
Jimmy Carter	1977-1981		1978	1979	1980	1981
Gerald R. Ford	1974-1977			1975	1976	1977

(callout: Select links to presidential addresses here)

20. In the speeches that you find at these links, you will find the president describing and defending various budget priorities. *Based on this review, come to a conclusion about two ways in which the incoming president will offer substantially new budget directions compared to the priorities of George W. Bush. Fill in the worksheet with brief details about your conclusion.*

21. Finally, you can learn a good deal from the response of the Congressional Budget Office (CBO) to the president's budget proposals. The CBO staff are professional budget analysts, hired by Congress to prepare an independent and non-partisan analysis of the president's budget numbers and priorities. To review their analysis, go to **www.cbo.gov** (you visited this site earlier in this exercise).

22. On the right hand side of the website, you will find a section called "Frequently Requested," looking like the screenshot on the page 71. You want to select the document called **"An Analysis of the President's Budgetary Proposals for Fiscal Year 2010."**

and Product Accounts

ord University

Spreadsheets for Selected Estimates and Projections

Glossary of Budgetary and Economic Terms

Frequently Requested

Stimulus Proposals

An Analysis of the President's Budgetary Proposals for Fiscal Year 2009
March 2008   html   pdf

The Budget and Economic Outlook: Fiscal Years 2008 to 2018
January 2008   html   pdf   data   charts   webcast

The Long-Term Budget Outlook
December 2007   html   pdf   data   webcast

Budget Options
February 2007   html   pdf   data

Analyses of Operations in Iraq and Afghanistan

> Look for the
> Fiscal Year 2010
> Budgetary
> Analysis

23. A lengthy analysis will open up for your review. You **don't** need to read all of this document for this exercise. All you are looking for are some details about how the president's new budget proposals will affect overall revenues/deficits, and how they will affect mandatory and discretionary spending levels. *Mandatory* spending is for things like Social Security and debt payments, which generally are not affected by who is the current president. *Discretionary* spending is for programs where spending can move up or down, depending on the current political priorities.

24. Details regarding these spending patterns are in chapter one of the CBO budget analysis, which is broken down into sections as seen in the screenshot below (you will be looking at the 2010 budget, not the 2009 budget). Scroll down to see the table of contents on your screen.

Contents

1

25. By reviewing the information found in chapter one, you will find details on the following points, helping you to fill in the worksheet:

- *Does the CBO predict the president's budget will create growing or shrinking budget deficits over the next five years?* (see table 1-1 in this chapter, and examine the section called "CBO's estimate of the president's budget for 2010"; see screenshot below).

- *Find one presidential policy proposal that will affect revenues, and briefly summarize how it will do so.* You can find this by simply clicking the link for "Policy Proposals That Affect Revenues" in the Table of Contents for chapter one (see screenshot on previous page).

- *Describe one presidential policy proposal that will affect mandatory spending.* Clicking "Policy Proposals That Affect Mandatory Spending" in the Table of Contents for chapter one.

- *Describe one presidential policy proposal that will affect discretionary spending.* Click "Policy Proposals That Affect Discretionary Spending" in the Table of Contents for chapter one.

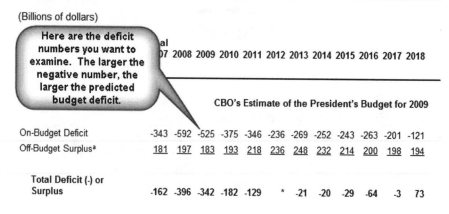

Table 1-1.

Comparison of Projected Deficits and Surpluses in CBO's Esti the President's Budget and in CBO's March 2008 Baseline

(Billions of dollars)

	2007	2008	2009	2010	2011	2012	2013	2014	2015	2016	2017	2018
On-Budget Deficit	-343	-592	-525	-375	-346	-236	-269	-252	-243	-263	-201	-121
Off-Budget Surplus[a]	181	197	183	193	218	236	248	232	214	200	198	194
Total Deficit (-) or Surplus	-162	-396	-342	-182	-129	*	-21	-20	-29	-64	-3	73

CBO's Estimate of the President's Budget for 2009

Done!

EXAMINING PRESIDENTIAL BUDGET PRIORITIES

1. Briefly summarize one key lesson that you learned from step 3.

2. What was the consequence of George W. Bush's budgets between 2001 and 2006, in terms of budget surpluses and deficits?

3. Summarize an interesting budget fact you have learned from the slide show you viewed in step 7.

4. Describe what you learned about budget tendencies in past decades, depending on who was president (step 12). Especially note one area of the budget (defense, agriculture, or health and human services) that seems to be especially affected by which party holds the presidency.

5. Do Democratic or Republican presidents tend to run bigger deficits (step 17)? Are you surprised? Why or why not?

6. Describe two ways in which the incoming president will offer new budget directions compared to the priorities of George W. Bush.

7. Does the Congressional Budget Office predict the president's budget will produce growing or shrinking deficits over the next five years?

8. Describe one presidential policy proposal that will affect overall revenues, and briefly summarize how it will do so.

9. Describe one presidential policy proposal that will affect mandatory spending and summarize how it will do so.

10. Describe one presidential policy proposal that will affect discretionary spending and summarize how it will do so.

Issue Six:
The President and the Pundits
Media Response to the New American President

According to a *PBS NewsHour* report on "The President and the Press," the First 100 Days of press coverage of the new presidency can have enduring importance: "The first 100 days [is] the so-called 'honeymoon' period for a new president and the press. It is often the time when the media takes the measure of a man, and helps create an image that can last for an entire presidency."[1]

Scholars have long known of something called the "primacy effect," which is simply the tendency of first impressions to last a long time. The first impression that one gets of the new president through media reporting can be expected to endure long into his presidency, for better or worse.[2] Presidents are, of course, well aware of this power of the media to shape enduring public impressions. That is why President Nixon dedicated immense staff time to viewing and categorizing all media reporting, in the newspapers and on television, and ordered his staff to prepare daily "media logs" that he could review to see exactly how much time he was receiving on the daily news and whether the news coverage was positive or negative in tone.[3]

In *The Audacity of Hope*, Barack Obama wrote about how even weekly or daily town hall meetings can never allow a public official to interact with

---

[1] "The President and the Press." A NewsHour with Jim Lehrer Transcript. April 25, 2001, http://www.pbs.org/newshour/bb/media/jan-june01/president_4-25.html (accessed October 10, 2008).

[2] R. Lance Holbert, et. al., "Primacy Effects of The Daily Show and National TV News Viewing: Young Viewers, Political Gratifications, and Internal Political Self-Efficacy." *Journal of Broadcasting and Electronic Media* (March 2007), http://findarticles.com/p/articles/mi_m6836/is_/ai_n25007511 (accessed on October 10, 2008).

[3] David Wise, "The President and the Press." *The Atlantic* (April 1973), www.theatlantic.com/doc/197304/nixon (accessed on October 10, 2008).

very many voters on a face-to-face basis. Inevitably, most voters will learn about officials through media reports. "I am who the media says I am," Obama concluded. "I stand for what the media says I stand for."[4]

In analyzing the leadership of the new president, therefore, it is important to examine the relationship between the president and the press during The First 100 Days. The First 100 Days is commonly called a "honeymoon period" for the president, meaning that the press is assumedly more likely to give the president favorable coverage during these hopeful early days of his presidency. But does the media, in fact, generally tend to offer positive coverage during this time? Specifically, how are they treating the new American president? Is most press coverage positive in tone, negative, or balanced and neutral? What about ideological bias? Some people are very concerned about alleged liberal bias in the mainstream media, while others allege a conservative bias to much news coverage. Can such bias be detected in the media coverage of the First 100 Days of the new presidency?

You will explore these questions in this exercise. You will review some of the historic trends in media coverage of The First 100 Days, allowing you to better compare today's coverage to patterns in the past. You will examine allegations of liberal and conservative bias in press coverage, and will draw your own conclusions. And you will categorize a series of news reports on the new president as positive, negative or neutral in tone, giving you some hard evidence with which to judge the relationship between the president and the press in this early "honeymoon period."

---

[4] Barack Obama, *The Audacity of Hope* (New York: Crown Press, 2006).

THE PRESIDENT AND THE PUNDITS

1. Begin your exploration of how the press treats the new president in his First 100 Days by reviewing how this press-president relationship played out during previous presidencies. Begin by viewing a short video clip from the *PBS NewsHour*, focused on President George W. Bush's relationship with the media during the First 100 Days of his presidency. Go to **www.pbs.org/newshour/bb/media/jan-june01/president_4-25.html.**

2. You will see links to view a video or read a transcript from the NewsHour report on the First 100 Days of the Bush presidency. **View or read the transcript of the program**.

3. *Use your worksheet to summarize one important lesson you learned from the program regarding the relationship between the president and the press during the First 100 Days.*

4. The First 100 Days is commonly called a "honeymoon period" for the president, meaning that the press is assumedly more likely to give the president favorable coverage during these hopeful early days of his presidency. Does the media, in fact, offer positive coverage during this time? Over the years, there have been several studies of this question. Researchers have viewed television reports and read articles produced during the First 100 Days of past presidencies, coded them as either positive, negative, or neutral in tone, and reported what they have found. You will explore these findings in the next steps.

5. The Center for Media and Public Affairs (CMPA) is a nonpartisan research and educational organization that conducts scientific studies of the news and entertainment media. The Center puts out studies of media coverage of the president, including coverage during the First 100 Days. To see their findings concerning how President George W. Bush was covered during his First 100 Days, go to **www.cmpa.com/files/media_monitor/01mayjun.pdf**.

6. A report appears, titled "The Disappearing Honeymoon: TV News Coverage of President George W. Bush's First 100 Days." Scan this report, and look for conclusions regarding the tone of media coverage of the president. Specifically, compare the First 100 Days of President George H.W. Bush, President Clinton, and President George W. Bush, and look for the percent of all news coverage on each president that had a positive tone. *Fill in this information on your worksheet* and notice the difference between the percent of positive coverage in 1988 (the first Bush presidency) and in 2000 (the second Bush presidency).

7. The Pew Research Center's Project for Excellence in Journalism also has studied press coverage during the first months of a new president. View their report at **www.journalism.org/node/312**.

8. You will see an executive summary of a report titled "The First 100 Days: How Bush Versus Clinton Fared in the Press." This report has similar, but different, findings from the Center for Media and Public Affairs report that you reviewed. On this executive summary page, you can see charts and summary analysis from the report. The right hand side of the page has chapter links to view the entire report. **You do NOT need to read the whole report.** Just look over the executive summary material on this page, and look at the charts. **Especially examine the chart titled "Tone of Coverage for Bush and Clinton."**

9. Use the chart to compare the percent of Bush and Clinton stories that were positive in tone during the first months of each presidency. *Fill in this information in your worksheet.*

10. Based on what you learn from the preceding studies, you can draw some initial conclusions about the tone of media coverage during the early days of a presidency. Examine the data that you filled in for question 2 of the worksheet, and notice whether the majority of coverage is positive in tone or not, and whether the trend since the first Bush presidency (1988) is toward more or less positive coverage.

11. Now that you have reviewed some of the trends in media coverage of past presidencies, you will move on to a review of how the current president is being covered in the media. Before you examine the overall tone of coverage (positive, negative, or neutral), you will explore some of the findings of media watchdog groups that are dedicated to unveiling ideological bias in the media.

12. Go to **www.mediaresearch.org**. You are at the homepage of the Media Research Center, a conservative media watchdog organization dedicated (in its own words) to "documenting, exposing and neutralizing liberal media bias."

13. This homepage includes a number of highlighted "alerts" about recent episodes of alleged liberal bias in the media. If any of the reports featured on the homepage relate to media coverage of the new president, **click the links to review up to three such reports**.

14. If there are not enough relevant reports highlighted on the homepage, **click the "Press Releases" button** in the menu on the left hand side of the page (in the "Publications and Analysis" section).

15. A list of press releases appears. **Search through this list and click the links to review several reports** on liberal media bias that relate to press coverage of the new president. **Between steps 13 and 15, you should review a total of at least 3 separate reports/allegations of liberal media bias.**

16. Does this short review persuade you that there may be systematic liberal media bias for or against the new president? *Summarize your thoughts on the worksheet.*

17. Now you will review allegations of conservative media bias. Go to **http://mediamatters.org.** This is the homepage of "Media Matters for America," an organization (in its own words) "dedicated to comprehensively monitoring, analyzing, and correcting conservative misinformation in the U.S. media."

18. This homepage includes a number of highlighted "alerts" about recent episodes of alleged conservative bias in the media. If any of the reports featured on the homepage relate to media coverage of the new president, **click the links to review the reports**.

19. If you do not find at least three relevant reports to review on the homepage, you can find additional reports on media coverage of the new president by **using the search box** to the top left of the page (type in the name of the current president). Alternatively, you can **click on the issues/topics button** in the menu bar on the top of the page, and look for relevant reports under the **"Government and Elections"** section.

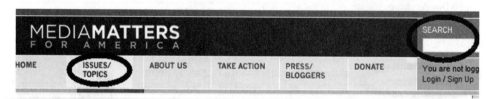

20. Review at least three episodes of alleged conservative media bias in reporting on the new president. Does this short review persuade you

that there may be systematic conservative media bias for or against the new president? *Summarize your thoughts on the worksheet.*

21. Now you will move on to investigating the overall tone of media coverage of the new president, updating the studies you reviewed in steps 5–10, earlier. Begin by returning to the Center for Media and Public Affairs (CMPA) at **www.cmpa.com**.

22. Click on the links on the menu bar at the top of this page for **"Press Releases"** and **"Media Monitor."**

23. Scan the document titles available at these two sections of the website and search for analysis of the tone of media coverage of the new presidency. When you find a promising title, **follow the link to read more of the report. You only need to scan a single report.**

24. *Use your worksheet to summarize what this CMPA report teaches about the overall tone of media coverage of the new president.* Does it seem that the new president is receiving very favorable or very harsh treatment in the media?

25. Finally, you can conduct some of your own "content analysis" of the tone of coverage of the new president. "Content Analysis" simply means that you watch or read news coverage and then analyze the meaning of its content. For this exercise, you will analyze some of the coverage of a leading cable news channel, CNN.

26. Go to **www.cnn.com**.

27. You can search CNN for news videos and other news on the new president. **Use the search box at the top of the page, and type in the**

name of the new president. You could also try typing in "First 100 Days" as a separate search and see what that returns. Above the search box, make sure you click the option to search **CNN "news"** or **CNN "videos,"** rather than the "web" option (see screenshot). **Choosing to search for CNN videos is the best strategy**; it will result in news clips that are the easiest to assess for their overall tone—since they will include both images and sound, in addition to the text of the report.

28. The search will return a number of videos or news reports on the new president. From this list, choose at least eight videos to view or news reports to read. After you read or view each report, assign it to a category: mostly positive in tone, mostly negative in tone, or balanced/neutral. You will have to use your own best judgment in assigning reports to the right category. Ask yourself whether the report leaves the reader with a positive or negative feeling about the president, or does it seem neutral or balanced? What images or adjectives are used in the reporting, and how does that shape the overall tone of the report? *Keep track of how many reports you put in each category (positive, negative, or neutral/balanced) and report this data on your worksheet.*

29. Based on your very small sample, do you conclude that CNN reporting on the new president tends to be mostly positive, mostly negative, or balanced/neutral? How does this compare to the findings of the studies you reviewed in steps 5–10? *Summarize your conclusions on the worksheet.*

Done!

THE PRESIDENT AND THE PUNDITS

1. Summarize a lesson from the *NewsHour* program on the relationship between the president and the press during the First 100 Days

2. According to CMPA and PEW reports (steps 6 and 9), what was the percent of news coverage that was positive in tone during the First 100 Days of Presidents George H.W. Bush, President Bill Clinton, and President George W. Bush?

	CMPA Report: % Positive	PEW Report: % Positive
George H.W. Bush		
Bill Clinton		
George W. Bush		

3. Does your review of Media Research Center material indicate that there may be a liberal bias to coverage of the new president? Explain.

4. Does your review of MediaMatters material indicate that there may be a conservative bias to coverage of the new president? Explain.

5. What does the CMPA report teach about the overall tone of media coverage of the new president: Is it very positive or very harsh?

6. Based on your own content analysis of eight CNN reports, how many were positive in tone, negative in tone, and neutral or balanced?

Positive Tone	Negative Tone	Neutral/Balanced

7. Does CNN reporting on the new president tend to be positive, negative, or balanced/neutral? How does this compare to the findings of the studies you reviewed in steps 5–10?

Across the globe, "anti-Americanism is extensive" and growing.[1] That is the conclusion of a 2007 worldwide public opinion poll of the Pew Global Attitudes Project. This poll, and many others, have documented that the global image of the United States has been in decline over the previous eight years, that President Bush has inspired more global distrust than any major world leader except Musharraf, and that even Russia's non-democratic President Putin was seen more favorably than the American president in 2008.[2] It is safe to say that the reputation of America and of its president has been somewhat tarnished in recent years.

Does it matter what the world thinks of America and its president? Amar Bakshi, a Fellow at the Center for International and Strategic Studies, thinks that it does. Here is how he describes the importance of maintaining a positive American image in the world.

> *America's image in the world is a key factor in keeping us safe, advancing our democratic ideals, and maintaining our competitive edge. Anti-Americanism directly weakens our national security and, at critical junctures, can damage our economic and political interests . . . For example, in 2003 the Turkish parliament reacted to public outcry and refused to grant America permission to open a northern front in Iraq. In Poland, public pressure made our missile defense shield a far tougher political sell for the nation's leaders. And in France low public opinion ratings for the U.S. and the war in Afghanistan make President Nicolas Sarkozy's job keeping French troops there harder each day.*

---

[1] Pew Global Attitudes Project, "Global Unease With Major World Powers" (June 27, 2007), http://pewglobal.org/reports/display.php?ReportID=256 (accessed on October 7, 2008).

[2] Ibid. See also Worldpublicopinion.org, "World Poll Finds Global Leadership Vacuum" (June 16, 2008), www.worldpublicopinion.org/pipa/pdf/jun08/WPO_Leaders_Jun08_pr.pdf (accessed on October 7, 2008).

Fareed Zakaria recounts a May 2007 exchange between Sarkozy and Condoleezza Rice. Rice asked Sarkozy, "What can I do for you?" And he replied, "Improve your image in the world. It's difficult when the country that is the most powerful, the most successful—that is, of necessity, the leader of our side—is one of the most unpopular countries in the world. It presents overwhelming problems for you and overwhelming problems for your allies."

. . . Among young Muslims, anti-Americanism provides a convenient rallying point for discontentment [and terrorist retaliation]. . . . If anti-American sentiments harden, young citizens around the world might opt for something new, another narrative that places [other countries] at the front of the emerging global order. This could impact where they go to study, work, and innovate, and, among the extreme, whether they decide to engage in violence against an old foe.

The task for the coming administrations is to convince world citizens that their successes and our successes are intertwined.[3]

There are good reasons for America to be concerned with its image in the world, and we can expect the new president to be attuned to how his leadership is playing in the world. America will show the world a new face for the first time in eight years in 2009, and it will undeniably have some sort of impact on world opinion. The First 100 Days of the new presidency will offer a unique moment when world opinion will be fluid, and especially responsive to new leadership, according to two former National Security Advisors, Zbigniew Brzezinski and Brent Scowcroft.[4] In this exercise, you will explore the state of world opinion regarding America and its president, both before and after the 2008 election. You will examine polls and news reporting from other countries and draw conclusions about whether the new president is using the First 100 Days the reshape America's image across the globe.

---

[3] Amar C. Bakshi, "Why World Views of America Matter" (undated, c. 2008), http://nextamerica.csis.org/node/563 (accessed on October 7, 2008).
[4] Zbigniew Brzezinski and Brent Scowcroft, *America and the World* (New York: BasicBooks, 2008) pp. 253–274.

THE PRESIDENT AND THE PLANET

1. To best understand how the current president is being viewed by people around the world, it is important to gain historical context by examining earlier world opinion regarding the previous president and about America in general. Understanding previous global attitudes about America and its president will help you to understand whether the current president is provoking a change in world opinion or not.

2. Begin your review of recent global attitudes about America and its president by going to **www.pbs.org/frontlineworld/election2008/**. You are taken to the "Election 2008: The World is Watching" section of PBS (public television). You can see a number of links to news videos covering the American 2008 election, including an "archives" link at the bottom of the page. Explore any of this material you wish.

3. When you are done exploring on your own, you need to find the fall Frontline 2008 report by Matthew Bell on "America's Image Abroad," a news report on the state of world opinion regarding America at that time. Return to the homepage at **www.pbs.org/frontlineworld/election2008/**. To find the Matthew Bell report, **use the search button** on the top of that page. **Fill in the following terms "Matthew Bell U.S. Image Abroad," and then hit "Search."**

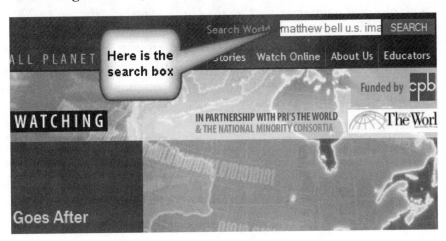

4. You will see links for the Frontline Election 2008 "The World is Watching" report. **Click one of those links and follow subsequent links for "The World's Matthew Bell reports."** The report is titled **"America's Image Abroad,"** and you may see a link with that title. The link you will follow to the final report may look like the screenshot below. The persistent link to go directly to the report should be **www.theworld.org/?q=node/21043**.

   When you get to the report, click the link to listen to it.

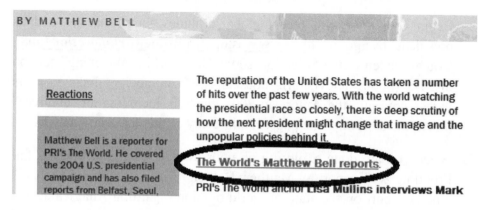

5. *Based on the Matthew Bell 2008 "America's Image Abroad" report that you just listened to, use your worksheet to summarize the general state of world opinion regarding the United States in the fall of 2008.*

6. For more information on global attitudes toward America, you can review reports found at the Pew Global Attitudes Project. This project is built on a series of worldwide public opinion surveys of almost 200,000 people in 54 countries. Go to the Global Attitudes Project homepage at **http://pewglobal.org/**.

7. You can see a wide range of interesting reports, charts and commentary on this homepage. To get to the data regarding worldwide attitudes toward America, click the **"reports"** button on the top of the page.

Pew Global Attitudes Project
A PewResearchCenter Project

HOME   ABOUT THE PROJECT   REPORTS   COMMENTARIES   DAT

About the Project   **Featured Reports**   Com

8. A list of reports appears. Look through the list for two reports:

- 06.27.07 "Global Unease With Major World Powers"

- 06.13.06 "America's Image Slips"

Click the links to review those reports. You DO NOT need to read the entire report. When you click the links, an executive summary of the report loads, together with key charts. That's all you have to look over, in order to answer the question in step 9, below.

If there is a link to a more recent report that seems to focus on global attitudes regarding the United States, you might want to click the link to review that report as well.

9. *Based on the data in these reports, use your worksheet to summarize the overall state of favorable or unfavorable world opinion toward the United States over the last several years. Provide one piece of data that is an example of this world opinion (for example, summarize Great Britain's changing U.S. favorability rating from 2000 to 2006).*

10. To deepen your understanding of the state of world opinion of America in the period preceding the 2008 election, review the results of a 2007 BBC (British Broadcasting Corporation) poll of 26,000 people in 25 countries. See the poll results at **http://news.bbc.co.uk/1/shared/bsp/hi/pdfs/23_01_07_us_poll.pdf**.

11. *Summarize the major conclusions of this BBC poll on your worksheet.*

12. Finally, you can review the general state of world confidence in the George W. Bush presidency, as compared to other world leaders, in a

2008 poll by the World Public Opinion organization. To see a press release on the results of this global "world leaders" poll, go to: **www.worldpublicopinion.org/pipa/pdf/jun08/WPO_Leaders_Jun_08_pr.pdf**.

13. *Summarize the major conclusion of this World Public Opinion poll on your worksheet.*

14. Now you have a good understanding of the state of world public opinion as the new president was coming into office. As you can see, the new president faces significant challenges in terms of inspiring the world with the case for U.S. leadership and values. You will now review some data about how world public opinion has or has not changed during the First 100 Days of the new presidency.

15. A great place to research world opinion on a variety of issues is the World Public Opinion website. Go to **www.worldpublicopinion.org**.

16. On this homepage, you see numerous links to recent polls, studies and analysis of world opinion on a variety of subjects. You may see a world public opinion poll on the leadership of the new president, or about America in general, highlighted on this front page. If so, click the link to review the poll or analysis.

17. To see archives of world polls and analysis relating to the current U.S. president that are available on **www.worldpublicopinion.org**, use the search button to the top right of the page. **Fill in the search box with the name of the current U.S. president and hit the "Go" button.** A list of polls and analysis will appear.

18. Select one or two links from this list to explore further. What do you learn about the state of overall world opinion regarding the new U.S. president? *Summarize your findings on the worksheet.*

19. Now return to the homepage at **www.worldpublicopinion.org**. On the left hand side of this page there are links to different regions of the world. **Pick a region that is interesting to you and click the button.** Scroll through the list of available studies and polling reports. Try to find one piece of analysis regarding how the new president and/or his policies are being received in this specific region. *Summarize your findings on the worksheet.*

20. Another way to analyze how the current president is perceived in the rest of the world is to review some of the coverage in the foreign press. The website **watchingamerica.com** provides a compendium of analysis about America collected from newspapers all across the world. Here is how the website describes the content on **watchingamerica.com**: *"WatchingAmerica reflects global opinion about the United States, helping Americans and non-Americans alike understand what the world thinks of current issues that involve the U.S. This is done by providing news and views about the United States published in other countries."*

21. Go to **www.watchingamerica.com**.

22. You will see all sorts of articles, grouped by region of the world. There are also links to more than a hundred world newspapers on the bottom of the page. To find world reporting on the new American president, **type the president's name in the search box on the top right of the page and hit "search."**

23. A list of articles appears. **Select two articles from this list** that appear interesting, in terms of shedding light on how different areas of the world are responding to the leadership of the new president. *Summarize what you learn from each of these articles on the worksheet.*

24. Finally, you can find additional reporting on the worldwide response to the new president at the website of "PRI's The World." This is the website of Public Radio International and includes reporting from the BBC and WGBH (Boston). Go to **www.theworld.org**.

25. When the website loads, you will see an option to use the search box (top right of page**). Type in the name of the current president and hit "Search." Review the available reports and select one piece of reporting on the worldwide response to the new president (or on the response of a specific country or region).** *Summarize what you learn from this report on your worksheet.*

26. What have you learned about the state of world opinion, both before and after the 2008 presidential election? *Use your worksheet to summarize your conclusions about how the current president is being received across the globe, and how that reception does or does not parallel the* **pre-election** *state of world opinion regarding America.*

Done!

THE PRESIDENT AND THE PLANET

1. Based on the "America's Image Abroad" report, summarize the state of world opinion regarding the United States in the fall of 2008.

2. Based on the Pew Global Attitudes Project that you reviewed in step 8, summarize the state of favorable or unfavorable world opinion toward the United States over the last several years. Provide one piece of data that is an example of this world opinion (for example, Great Britain's changing U.S. favorability rating from 2000 to 2006).

3. Summarize the major conclusions of the 2007 BBC poll that you reviewed in step 10 of this exercise.

4. Summarize the conclusions of the 2008 World Public Opinion poll.

5. Summarize the findings of the World Public Opinion poll or analysis that you reviewed concerning the newly elected president (step 18).

6. Describe how the newly elected president is being perceived in one region of the world, based on the material you reviewed in step 19.

7. What do you learn from the first article you reviewed at **www.watchingamerica.com**?

8. What do you learn from the second article you reviewed at **www.watchingamerica.com**?

9. What do you learn about how the president is being received in the world from the report you reviewed at PRI's "The World"?

10. Summarize your conclusions about how the current president is being received across the globe, and how that reception does or does not parallel the **pre-election** state of world opinion regarding America.

Everyone loves a winner. Maybe that helps explain why the percent of people approving of a newly elected president invariably starts out substantially higher than the percent of people who actually voted for that president. Even presidents narrowly elected in bitter November elections (such as Carter or Nixon) commonly enjoy approval ratings above 60% during their first months in office. This period of time in the early months of a new presidency, when much of the public seems to wrap its arms around the new president, and when the press and the Congress commonly refrain from attacking the president and are more supportive of his leadership, is called the president's "honeymoon period." It is a time of national goodwill and optimism about what the new president might bring to the nation.

Public approval ratings during the presidential honeymoon are commonly very high, compared to approval ratings that most presidents post later in their administration. President Johnson began his presidency with a 75% approval rating—by the end of his presidency, approval ratings were in the low 40s. President Carter started with a 70% approval rating, and ended with approval in the low 30s. President George W. Bush started in 2001 with approval ratings around 50%, and by the end of his presidency in the fall of 2008, his approval ratings were only about 25%.[1]

Public approval of presidential leadership has been tracked since the 1930s, when polling leader George Gallup began to measure and report on it regularly. In these tracking polls over the years, it has become clear that almost all presidents end their presidency far less popular than when they began it. A minority of presidents, namely FDR, Reagan and Clinton, were able to end their presidencies more popular than when they began

---

[1] "Comparing Past Presidential Performance," Roper Center Public Opinion Archives. http://webapps.ropercenter.uconn.edu/CFIDE/roper/presidential/webroot/presidential_rating.cfm (accessed October 3, 2008).

them. It seems that the high hopes and soaring optimism that accompanies a new presidency are inevitably let down and depressed by the inevitable compromises, battles and failures that every president faces in the complicated American political system. Also, the public simply tires of the leadership of a single president and his party over time and becomes ready for something new.

But the predictable decline in presidential popularity, often culminating in an ineffective and unpopular "lame duck" president by the end of his term, is eons away (politically) during that early honeymoon period when presidential popularity soars. For this reason, the honeymoon period, which overlaps with the First 100 Days of the new presidency, is a critical time for presidential action—a time when the new president has the most leeway to lay the foundation for new policies, secure approval for his nominees, and shape the political landscape for the four years to come. So it is important to pay attention to presidential approval ratings during the honeymoon period—as they are source of much of the president's "political capital" and much of his power as he seeks to move Congress and the nation more broadly into supporting his proposals and way of thinking.

In this exercise, you will examine historic trends in presidential approval ratings. You will also look in detail at the current president's approval rating during this First 100 Days period and will examine whether the president's popularity varies by region of the country. In the end, you will offer some thoughts on why presidential approval trends tend to move in the direction they do over time.

PRESIDENTIAL APPROVAL RATINGS

1. You will begin your study of presidential approval ratings by gaining some historical perspective on how the public tends to rate its presidents, and how these ratings change over time. The Roper Center of the University of Connecticut maintains public opinion archives over the last 60-plus years. To examine their historic data archives on presidential approval ratings, go to **www.ropercenter.uconn.edu**.

2. You are taken to the homepage of the Roper Center. On the top of the page is a menu button for **"Data Access."** Click this button for a dropdown menu of options. On this menu, click the option for **"Presidential Approval."**

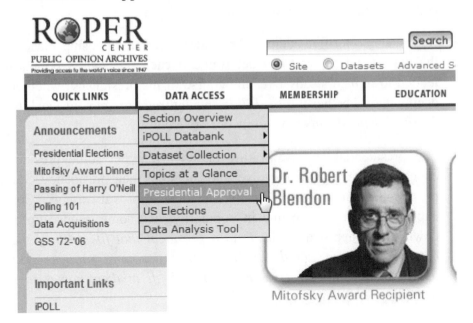

3. You are taken to a section of the Roper center that provides data on the latest job performance ratings of the president. Look over the ratings to get a sense of where the president currently stands with the public.

4. When you are done looking over current presidential performance ratings, scroll down the page to a section titled **"Comparing Past Presidential Performance."** In this section, you can see a list of the

highest approval rating and lowest approval rating scored by each president since Franklin Roosevelt. Examine this list and you can see that the same president posted the highest ever approval rating, and *also* posted the lowest approval rating ever. *Fill in your worksheet with the name of this "roller-coaster" president.*

5. The presidents' names in the **"Comparing Past Presidential Performance"** section are clickable. When you click a name, approval rating data and a timeline chart load for that president. This data can help you with historical perspective on approval rating trends.

6. Begin by clicking the name of **President George W. Bush**. When the page loads, explore the data and especially examine the chart at the bottom of the page that shows you how President George W. Bush's approval ratings changed over time.

7. Repeat step 6 for five additional presidents of your choosing. Based on the data you find, you can determine if each president's popularity tended to remain steady over the course of his presidency, whether it declined, or whether it rose. *Fill in this information on your worksheet for the five presidents that you choose to study.*

8. The presidential approval rating charts teach that some presidents experience rising popularity over the course of their presidency. Some presidents remain fairly steady in their approval ratings. Some experience a steady decline in popularity, and some bounce up and down in the approval polls. *Find a president that fits each of these categories (rising popularity, constantly declining ratings, steady approval, and up-and-down ratings) and fill in their names in the worksheet.*

9. One president's popularity far outpaced most others. His presidential approval ratings never dipped below 56%, and disapproval ratings sometimes were as low as 6%. Which president was that? *Fill in the answer in your worksheet.*

10. Based on the information in these charts, what is the most common trend in presidential popularity over the course of their presidency? Look over the data and ponder whether presidential approval ratings tend usually to go up over time, or to go down.

11. Another good site for approval rating research is the American Presidency Project of John Woolley and Gerhard Peters. View their data at **www.presidency.ucsb.edu/data/popularity.php**.

12. At this page, you can see a list of all presidents since Franklin Roosevelt, together with their approval ratings over time. There is also a color bar beside each president's rating, with blue standing for high approval ratings, and red standing for low ratings. You can scroll down the list of presidents and see which ones tend to stay "in the blue" (high ratings), which ones shift from blue to red, and other such trends. Spend some time scrolling down the information on this page.

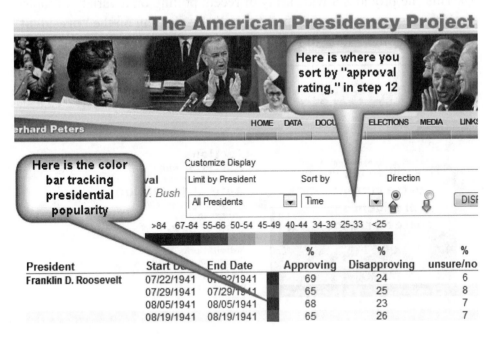

13. After looking over the information on this page, you can sort the data by highest and lowest approval ratings. In the menu boxes above the data, you can see an option to sort data by "presidents," "% approving," or "% disapproving." See the screenshot above for

guidance on where this menu box is located. **In this menu box, select the option to sort the data by "% approving," and then click the "Display" button to the right.** The data updates.

14. The data is now arranged in order, from the lowest recorded approval ratings to the highest ratings. This data parallels, but isn't exactly the same, as the polling data reported on the Roper site that you visited earlier in this exercise. From the rankings, you can determine which two presidents posted the consistently lowest approval ratings, and which two presidents posted the consistently highest ratings. *Fill in that information on the worksheet.*

15. Now that you have built some historical knowledge you can better understand and contextualize the current president's approval ratings. To examine the current ratings, go to **www.pollingreport.com**.

16. This site provides a wide array of recent polling on a variety of topics. You can see presidential approval polls by clicking on the **"president"** link under the **"State of the Union"** section.

17. A page will load with links to explore recent **"job ratings"** and **"favorability ratings"** of the current president. Follow those links and

estimate the average approval rating of the president in the last several polls. *Fill in this information on your worksheet.*

18. The president often has to work with Congress and sometimes has to battle Congress to advance his priorities. In that process of working with and battling Congress, it is important to know whether Congress is more or less popular than the president, and how great the difference is. If a president has very high approval ratings, and Congress has very low approval ratings, it may enhance the president's power in bargaining with Congress. To explore Congressional approval ratings, return to the homepage of **www.pollingreport.com.** The second link in the "State of the Union" section is for "**Congress**" (you can see it below the "President Bush" link in the previous screenshot), which you can follow to find Congressional approval rating.

19. Click the "**Congress**" link and explore the average Congressional approval ratings over the last several polls. *Fill in this information on your worksheet.* Think over the political implications of whether the president is substantially more popular than Congress at this point, or not.

20. Finally, you will explore state by state presidential approval ratings. Is the president's popularity generally equal across the nation, or is he much more popular in some regions than others? To answer that question, you will explore presidential popularity in states that represent the Northeast, the South, the Midwest, the Rocky Mountains and the Pacific Coast.

21. For state polls, go to **www.presidentpollsusa.com.** A list of state-level presidential approval polls appears. You can also scroll down to a map on the page, below which are links for state-level approval polls. You can click on any of the state names to get the most recent polls from this site.

22. Use this list of states to find a state poll in each of the five regions of the country: the Northeast (1), the Midwest (2), the South (3), the

Rocky Mountain West (4), and the Pacific Coast (5). The map below shows which states fall into which regions.

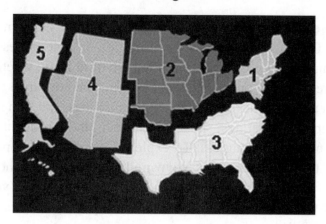

23. *Fill in your worksheet with the percent of people approving of the job the president is doing for* **one state** *in each region of the country.* If you cannot find a state poll from any of the regions, leave that space blank in your worksheet.

24. Based on this data, what can you conclude about the president's "geography of approval?" Is the president's approval fairly equal across the nation, or is there a region with unusually high or low approval ratings? *Share your thoughts on the worksheet.*

25. You have learned that the usual trend over time is for a president's predictably high "honeymoon" approval ratings to steadily decline over time. Why do you think most presidents experience lower and lower approval ratings over the years of their presidency? *Share your thoughts on the worksheet.*

Done!

PRESIDENTIAL APPROVAL RATINGS

1. Which president enjoyed both the highest and lowest public approval ratings ever recorded?

2. List five presidents and describe whether public approval ratings rose or declined, when comparing the beginning and ends of their terms.

President's Name	Did Approval Rating Rise, Remain Steady, or Decline Over Time?

3. Fill in the chart below with a president who fits the category.

	President's Name
Steadily Rising Approval Rating	
Steadily Declining Approval Rating	
Relatively Steady Approval Rating	
Up and Down Approval Rating	

4. Which president consistently enjoyed the most high approval ratings throughout his presidency?

5. Fill in the information below.

	President's Names
2 Presidents with Consistently Lowest Approval Ratings	
2 Presidents with Consistently Highest Approval Ratings	

6. What is the recent public approval rating of the current president?

7. What is the recent public approval rating of the Congress?

8. Fill in the information below.

Region of the Country	**State**	**President's Approval Rating**	**Is president's support uniform, or does it vary by region?**
Northeast			
Midwest			
South			
Rocky Mountains			
Pacific Coast			

9. Why might most presidents experience declining approval over time?

ISSUE NINE:
NEW PRESIDENT, NEW FOREIGN POLICY?

Presidents have perhaps their greatest ability to shape national policy in the realm of foreign policy. Why is that? For one, it has been said that "politics stops at the water's edge," which means that the public, the media and members of Congress are less likely to criticize a president and demonstrate national disunity on matters involving other countries. Second, the president has unique constitutional powers over foreign policy, such as the sole negotiator of treaties and commander in chief of the armed forces. Third, the need for energy and unity in responding to international crises has led the president to become prominent in dealing with international matters. For such reasons, some have concluded that there are really "two presidencies"—the domestic affairs presidency and the foreign policy presidency, with the foreign policy president having far more stature and power than the domestic policy president.[1]

Americans today seem ready for vigorous presidential leadership in the realm of foreign affairs—and they want that leadership to fundamentally change previous foreign policy directions. A 2008 poll by the Chicago Council for Global Affairs found a desire for a new course in American foreign policy. The poll showed a strong desire for a new president to improve the U.S. international reputation, to work more closely with America's allies, and to talk more directly and use more diplomacy with enemies.[2] Voters want change in foreign policy—but will the "foreign policy" president deliver these significant foreign policy changes? What are some of the vital tools of presidential foreign policy making, and how is the new president using them?

Some of those tools include the presidential foreign policy team. That team includes the secretary of state, presiding over an army of thousands of diplomatic bureaucrats. The secretary of state's job is to conduct

---

[1] Aaron Wildavsky, "The Two Presidencies," *Trans-Action* 4 (December 1966): 7–14.
[2] Chicago Council on Global Affairs, "Americans Support Major Changes in U.S. Foreign Policy" (September 22, 2008), www.thechicagocouncil.org/media_press_room_detail.php?press_release_id=86 (accessed on October 14, 2008).

diplomatic relations with other nations and serve as a key advisor to the president on foreign policy issues. The foreign policy team also includes the secretary of defense, who oversees the military and presides over a budget larger than the budget of most entire nations.[3] Another key member of the team is the national security advisor, whose job is to coordinate America's foreign and military policies, and to advise the president on foreign affairs. By choosing people for these jobs who bring unique vision and priorities to their tasks, the new president begins the task of putting his imprint on American foreign policy.

Other tools of foreign policy include the president's treaty-making powers, as only the president can negotiate treaties (although the Senate must approve them). Presidents can also use a tool called "executive agreements." Like treaties, executive agreements bind America to certain courses of action vis-à-vis other nations—though they do not require Senate consent. Many of these agreements concern trivial matters (such as landing rights for airplanes), but they are sometimes used for fundamental matters (e.g., Reagan authorized military actions, Bush expanded the war on drugs, and Clinton expanded free trade using these agreements). Each year, hundreds of these agreements are unilaterally entered into by the president—90% of all foreign agreements are based on executive agreements, not treaties—thereby advancing the president's foreign policy goals without worrying about whether the Senate approves.

In this exercise, you will explore these various aspects of presidential foreign policy making. You will examine public opinion on foreign policy directions, explore some policy directions of the new president, and examine the president's use of both treaties and executive agreements. In the end, you will have a more informed answer to the question of whether the new president has brought American a new foreign policy.

---

[3] George Edwards III, et. al., *Government in America: People, Politics and Policy* (New York: Pearson Longman, 2008), p. 620.

NEW PRESIDENT, NEW FOREIGN POLICY?

1. Will a new U.S. president mean a new U.S. foreign policy? Polls show that people expect new directions in foreign policy, and scholars have often argued that Congress rarely constrains the president's foreign policy making, because of the notion that the president is supposed to be the singular head of state in dealing with foreign nations, and because "politics stops at the water's edge." But how much room does a president really have to reshape foreign policy, and what kinds of changes can he set into motion in his First 100 Days?

2. Not everyone believes that a president can set a fundamentally new policy course upon taking office. Presidents are prisoners of the policies of their predecessors (including the wars, and the global friends and enemies that the new president inherits). They are also limited by enduring public opinion about America's special role in the world, and by the events of history itself, which constrain presidential choices. To see how one historian talks about these constraints, go to **http://therealnews.com**.

3. You are at the homepage of a viewer-supported television news site, providing in-depth independent journalism. **Use the search box on this site (top right of page) to type in the key words "Gareth Porter"** (Gareth Porter is a historian and journalist who has commented about the foreign policy constraints facing the new president). **Then hit "search."**

4. A list of Gareth Porter videos appears. Scroll through this list and look for the video dated October 5, 2008, titled "Will a New U.S. President Mean a New Foreign Policy." **Click the link to view this short video.** As you watch this video, think about why the summary to the interview posted on this site says that Porter believes that "neither [McCain nor Obama] truly represent a clean break from the legacy created by the Bush administration."

5. What are the core points made by Porter in this interview, especially regarding the likelihood of the new president bringing a new vision and new policies to American foreign policy? *Summarize your thoughts on the worksheet.*

6. The journalist and historian in the interview was skeptical of the ability of the new president to deliver fundamental foreign policy change. But what do American citizens think about this topic? Do they WANT the current president to lead the nation in fundamentally new ways, as compared to the last eight years of foreign policy? You can get good insight on this question by reviewing the 2008 "Global Views" survey of the Chicago Council on Global Affairs.

7. Go to **www.thechicagocouncil.org**.

8. You are at the website of a non-partisan organization that works on opinion polls and policy analysis related to global issues. To see the results from a 2008 poll that this group did on American foreign policy attitudes, go to the **"Studies and Conferences"** button in the menu bar on the left hand side of the screen. A pop-up menu will appear. In that menu, roll your mouse over **"Public Opinion Survey."** Another menu will appear, and in that menu you should click on the option for **"Previous Surveys."** See screenshot on next page for guidance.

THE **CHICAGO COUNCIL**
ON GLOBAL AFFAIRS

Public Audience   **Individual Members**   **President's Circle**   C

Login

The Chicago Council

Programs

Studies & Conferences

Global Chicago

Special Events

Home > Current Survey

Current Survey|

Public Opinion Study - Global Views 2008
For its 2008 Public Opinion Study, The Chicago Council on Glo   U.
                                                                                     des
Public Opinion Survey >   Overview   s in
Task Forces   >   Current Survey   n S
Conferences   Previous Surveys
the fall of 2008.

9. In the list of surveys that appear, look for a survey titled **"Public Opinion Study—Global Views 2008." Click the link to view this survey.**

10. A summary page appears, summarizing the different parts of this poll. Scroll down the page to the section titled "**American Attitudes on U.S. Foreign Policy." Click the link for the "Press Release"** for this survey (see screenshot).

American Attitudes on U.S. Foreign Policy
On Monday, September 22, 2008, The Chicago Council on Global Affairs release findings on American attitudes toward a number of important foreign policy issue findings show the American public is concerned about the country's standing in t favors major changes in U.S. foreign policy.

- Americans believe the ability of the United States to achieve its foreign p decreased over the last few years and they think improving America's st world should be a very important goal of U.S. foreign policy;
- Americans support a number of changes in foreign policy including talkin making a deal with Iran, setting a timetable to withdraw forces from Iraq against terrorist groups operating in Pakistan, participating in a new clima treaty, and generally pursuing a more multilateral approach to U.S. forei
- While they favor policy changes, Americans are still committed to a robu presence in the world;

Full Report (PDF)
Press Release

11. **Read the press release.** According to this poll, what kind of changes do Americans want to see in U.S. foreign policy? *Provide your answer on the worksheet.*

12. Now you will move on to investigating the ways in which the new president is or is not pursuing fundamentally new directions in foreign policy. A key to understanding a president's foreign policy vision is to examine the foreign policy team he has assembled. What do the president's key advisors believe, and do they represent a shift from the thinking of the previous president?

13. To investigate this question, first **compile the names of three key foreign policy advisors to the new president: the secretary of state, the secretary of defense, and the national security advisor.** You can find these names with a simple Google search, or by going to **www.whitehouse.gov** and following links to see members of the president's cabinet.

14. Now that you have these three names, conduct a Google search using the name of the current secretary of state AND the name of the secretary of state under George W. Bush (Condoleezza Rice). Type in a search phrase such as **"[name of new secretary of state] different Condoleezza Rice."**

15. Review the links that appear and look for one promising article that talks about how the current and past secretary of state are different and/or similar. *When you are done reading the article, summarize its key points on your worksheet.*

16. **Repeat this same process,** comparing the current secretary of defense to the secretary of defense under Bush (EITHER Robert Gates or Donald Rumsfeld), and comparing the current national security advisor to the national security advisor under Bush (Stephen Hadley).

If you are having trouble finding good short articles to review, you might try different search terms such as:

- "[current secretary of state] different from Condoleezza Rice"

- "[current secretary of state] versus Condoleezza Rice"

- "[current secretary of state] new directions"

- "[current secretary of state] same as Condoleezza Rice"

- "[current secretary of state] stay the course"

17. *Summarize what you learn about each of these positions on your worksheet.*

18. The lead foreign policy advisor to the president is the secretary of state. The job of the State Department is to conduct the foreign affairs of the United States and manage its external relations. You can investigate the current priorities and philosophy of the State Department by going to **www.state.gov.**

19. You are at the home page of the Department of State. On this homepage, you will see links to videos, issue briefs, press conferences and vital news of the day. Look through these offerings and choose a link that seems to report on an important initiative or expression of vision by the State Department. **Click one link and review the information you find there.**

20. *Summarize what you learn about the actions or philosophy of the new Department of State on your worksheet.*

21. Another tool that the president uses to pursue his foreign policy agenda is a formal treaty that binds America (and other nations) into certain courses of action and that must be ratified by the U.S. Senate, in accordance with Constitutional rules. Treaties are one of the most formal ways that a president can announce to the nation and the world

his foreign policy vision, and they are serious and enduring declarations of a nation's goals and priorities.

22. To review some of the treaties that the new president has already advanced, go to **http://www.state.gov/s/l/treaty/**. You are at the webpage of the Department of State that reports on the nation's "Treaty Affairs." You will see all sorts of tools to explore the state of America's treaty relations. All you will do for this exercise is review the **"Highlights"** section of the page that provides an overview of treaties recently submitted to Congress.

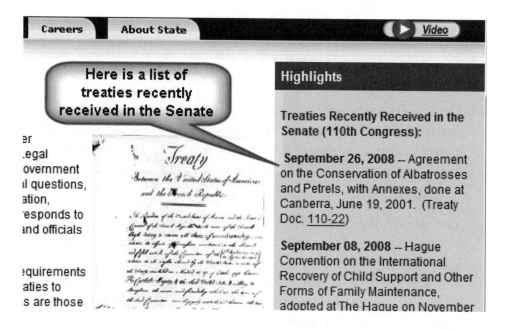

23. **Look on the right hand side of the page for the "Highlights" section.** Examine the kinds of treaties that the president has recently negotiated, if any. You will see a link that you could follow to review the text of the entire treaty, but you needn't do that now. Just read over the short title and description of the treaties in the "Highlights" section and think about what these treaties indicate about foreign policy goals of the president. *On your worksheet, summarize **one** lesson that you*

have learned about the president's foreign policy goal(s) from the treaty that you reviewed. If there is no recent treaty, skip this step.

24. Though the Constitution envisions that most foreign policy agreements with foreign nations would be treaties, negotiated by the president and enacted with the consent of the Senate, the fact is that about 90% of all agreements with foreign nations are unilaterally "imposed" by the president through the tool known as an executive agreement. An executive agreement binds nations to certain actions, just like a treaty—but it usually is much more narrow in scope and it doesn't require the consent of the Senate.

25. How often is the current president using executive agreements as a tool of foreign policy, and what kinds of agreements is he entering into? The chart below shows the frequency of executive agreements being used by previous presidents, which you will compare against the executive agreement rate of the current president.

Type of International Agreements: Treaties and Executive Agreements by Administration, 1977–1996

Presidential Term	Treaties	Executive Agreements	Total	Agreements Percentage of Total
Carter	56	1,098	1,154	95.1
Reagan I	58	965	1,023	94.3
Reagan II	48	605	653	92.6
G. H. W. Bush	58	569	627	90.7
Clinton I	80	667	747	89.3
Total	300	3,904	4,204	92.9

Source: Kiki Caruson and Victoria A. Farrar-Myers, "Promoting the President's Foreign Policy Agenda." *Presidential Research Quarterly* 60.4 (2007): 631–644.

26. Notice that presidents average about 150–200 executive agreements a year (while only averaging 15–20 formal treaties a year). Since you are completing this exercise about one-quarter of the way into the new president's first year in office, he should have issued 40–50 executive orders already, if he is to maintain the yearly pace of his predecessors. In the next step, you will investigate whether the new president is ahead of pace, on pace, or behind pace in his use of this unilateral tool of foreign policy direction.

27. Go to **www.state.gov/s/l/treaty/caseact/**. You are at the section of the Department of State's webpage where that Department reports on the nature of any international agreement, other than a treaty, to which the United States is a party (i.e., executive agreements).

28. On the left hand side of the page, you see a menu bar with links that you can click to see agreements by year. **Click on the link for "2009,"** and you will see a list of international agreements signed into force by the new president.

29. Scroll through that list and **count the total number of agreements entered into by the new president**. Only count agreements dated January 20, 2009, or later (inauguration day for the president). If the new president is to replicate the pace of his predecessors, he should have around 40–50 executive agreements at this point. *Use your worksheet to note how many agreements you counted.*

30. Each agreement has a short description and a link to read more about the agreement. Choose ONE agreement that seems non-trivial and interesting to you. **Click the link and read more about the agreement.** You don't have to read the entire agreement, but scan enough of it to understand its thrust. What do you learn about the president's foreign policy priorities from this agreement? *Summarize your thoughts on the worksheet.*

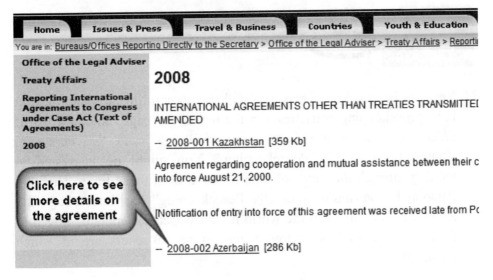

31. Another way the president shapes foreign policy is through influencing America's "peacekeeping" operations in the world. Peacekeeping operations include dedicating funding and troops to United Nations peacekeeping missions (such as in Kosovo or the Ivory Coast), or funding non-UN led peacekeeping efforts such as operations in Darfur and Somalia. Has the new president tended to continue the peacekeeping levels of the previous president, or has American

funding and personnel commitments to peacekeeping operations changed substantially?

32. You can investigate such questions by going to **www.stimson.org/fopo**. This organization tracks peacekeeping operations across the world and U.S. contributions to those efforts.

33. You will be at a "Future of Peace Operations" page. Scroll down this page to a button titled **"U.S. Policy."** Click the link to **"READ MORE."**

UN REFORM » The program has assessed the implementation of recommendations from the "Brahimi Report," a landmark UN publication calling for peacekeeping reform. Other research addresses the economic impact of peace operations on host nations.
READ MORE »

US POLICY » The program tracks US policy towards peace operations, including the funding of UN missions and military training programs. The program has also examined ___ of the International Criminal Court within the US military.
READ MORE »

34. You will be at a page where you will see several links to data tracking U.S. peacekeeping activities. On the top of the page, among a list of links, are links to "US Peacekeeping Funding," and "US Personnel Contributions to UN Peacekeeping." You might be interested in looking through the kinds of data found at both those links. The "US Personnel Contributions to UN Peacekeeping" has interesting data about what countries in the world have UN peacekeepers deployed to them and shows how many American peacekeepers are in which countries.

Tracking US Peace Operations Policy

🖶 Printer friendl

Below are resources for tracking US policy relevant to international peace and stability operations. Past program analysis in this area also includes an examination of views on the International Criminal Court within the US military and among policy makers.

US Peacekeeping Funding | Hill Policy Tracking | Congressional Testimony | US Personnel Contributions to UN Peacekeeping | US Views on the International Criminal Court | Archives

35. For this exercise, you will only need to follow the link for **"US Peacekeeping Funding." Click that link, or just scroll down the page to the "US Peacekeeping Funding" section.**

36. You see several options for tracking U.S. funding of peacekeeping efforts. You will examine U.S. funding trends for non-UN related activities here, since funding for UN-led activities is guided more by general UN rules and requests and less by specific presidential leadership. Non-UN led peacekeeping efforts are funded by America's **Peacekeeping Operations (PKO) Account, so click the link to that account** (see screenshot).

US Peacekeeping Funding

FOPO tracks the following US accounts within the State Department budget that are relevant fo peacekeeping:

Contributions to International Peacekeeping Activities (CIPA) Account

Peacekeeping Operations (PKO) Account

The program also tracks the Congressional "cap" on US contributions to UN peace operations.

37. You will see a list of links for US Funding to non-UN led peacekeeping efforts in different fiscal years (FY) (for example, FY08 and FY09). **Click on the links for "Info on FY08 PKO Funding" and "Info on FY09 PKO Funding"** to see how much funding was originally authorized for spending on such things as Darfur and Somalia peacekeeping in these two years (the last two years governed by Bush funding requests in the previous years).

PKO: US FUNDING FOR VOLUNTARY PEACEKEEPING ACTIVITIES

PKO Overview | FY09 Annual Appropriations

Info on FY08 PKO Funding

Info on FY07 PKO Funding

Info on the Contributions to International Peacekeeping Activities (CIPA) Account

PDF Version of this page available here

(Some links on this page will take you off the Stimson site.)

38. When you click the "Info on FY08 PKO Funding" link, you will see a chart appear (you may have to scroll down the page to see it), which

has the original "Administration Request" for 2008 peacekeeping funding (a request made in February of 2007).

FY08 Funding

	Administration Request	House Approved Level	Senate Appro
FY08 Annual Appropriations	$221.2 million (Feb. 07)	$293.2 million (Jun. 07)	$273.2 mi (Jun. 07)
FY08 Supplemental Appropriations	$0 (Oct. 07)		

39. Note the level of funding originally requested by the administration in 2007. You don't want to focus on the amount of money finally approved, nor on supplemental appropriations—as you want to compare the Bush administration's original request of peacekeeping funding to the new president's original request for peacekeeping funding this year.

40. After you have noted the original funding request for FY08, return to the screen that you were at in step 37, and do the same thing for FY09. Jot these two figures down on scrap paper—they are the last two years of Bush funding requests.

41. Now return to the screen you were at in step 37 (the screen where links to funding in different fiscal years appears). **Click on the link to "FY 10 Annual Appropriations,"** which should be right above the link for "FY09 PKO Funding" that you followed in the steps above. This FY10 link will take you to the original peacekeeping budget request submitted by the new president. If there is no such link and the new president has not yet submitted a funding request for peacekeeping operations, skip this step.

42. Is the amount requested significantly higher, lower, or about the same as peacekeeping budgets originally requested by President Bush for FY08 and FY09? *Include your answer on the worksheet.*

43. Finally, you will review a bit of what the president himself has to say on the subject of foreign affairs. Every week, the president makes dozens of speeches, gives short remarks, holds press conferences, and the like. All of these events and speeches are transcribed and made available online at **www.gpoaccess.gov/wcomp/**. Go there now.

44. This "Weekly Compilation of Presidential Documents" page has a search box about a third of the way down the page. In that search box type in the search phrase **"War on Terror,"** and select **"Submit."**

Weekly Compilation of Presidential Documents: Main Page

The Weekly Compilation of Presidential Documents is published every Monday and is the official publication of presidential statements, messages, remarks, and other materials released by the White House Press Secretary. Published by the Office of the Federal Register (OFR), National Archives and Records Administration (NARA), the Weekly Compilation of Presidential Documents first began in 1965 and is available on *GPO Access* from 1993 forward. More.

2008 (Volume 44) Compilation Only

- Search: (ex: "page 75626", "32 CFR 58", "railroad retirement board" AND benefits)

  | war on terror | | Submit | [Search Tips] |

- Browse the 2008 Compilation

---

45. A list of documents and speeches delivered by the president that touch on the War on Terror appears. Choose ONE of the speeches or remarks that look interesting to you and click the link to read the text of the speech or remarks.

46. What do you learn about the president's foreign policy vision and priorities from this speech? *Summarize your thoughts on your worksheet.*

47. Based on what you have learned in all the preceding steps in this exercise, what do you conclude about whether or not the new president is leading this nation in a fundamentally new foreign policy direction? *Summarize your final conclusion on your worksheet.*

Done!

NEW PRESIDENT, NEW FOREIGN POLICY?

1. What are the core points made by Gareth Porter in this interview, especially regarding the likelihood of the new president bringing a new vision and new policies to American foreign policy?

2. According to the Chicago Council on Global Affairs poll, what kind of changes do Americans want to see in U.S. foreign policy?

3. What are some key differences or similarities between the views of the new secretary of state and C. Rice, the outgoing secretary?

4. What are some key differences or similarities between the views of the new secretary of defense and the outgoing secretary?

5. What are some key differences or similarities between the views of the new national security advisor and the last one?

6. What do you learn about the foreign policy of the new president from the news and/or reports that you view at the homepage of the Department of State?

7. *Summarize* **one** *lesson that you have learned about the president's foreign policy goal(s) from the treaty or treaties that you reviewed.*

8. How many executive agreements did you count in step 29?

9. What did you learn about the president's foreign policy in the single executive agreement that you reviewed in more detail?

10. Is the level of peacekeeping funds requested by the new president significantly higher, lower, or about the same as peacekeeping budgets originally requested by President Bush for FY08 and FY09?

11. What did you learn about the president's foreign policy vision and priorities from the speech that you reviewed?

12. Based on what you have learned throughout this exercise, what do you conclude about whether or not the new president is leading this nation in a fundamentally new foreign policy direction?

ISSUE TEN: THE HONEYMOON EFFECT
PRESIDENTIAL SUPPORT IN CONGRESS

President Johnson advised future presidents to focus above all at pushing their agenda through Congress during their very first year. "You've got to give it all you can, that first year . . . before they start worrying about themselves. . . . You can't put anything through when half of Congress is thinking how to beat you."[1]

In America's system of divided powers, a president cannot govern alone. How Congress votes on measures desired by a president is critical in determining just how successful a president is as a leader, and there may be no more important time than the First 100 Days in getting presidential measures passed. As a leading textbook of American politics notes:

> Because presidents generally experience declining support for policies they advocate throughout their terms, it is important that a president proposes key plans early in his administration, during the honeymoon period, a time when the good-will toward the president often allows a president to secure passage of legislation that he would not be able to gain at a later period.[2]

There are many reasons a president can expect higher success rates in Congress during his First 100 Days than in later years. National goodwill following a presidential election extends into Congress, and the sense of a "mandate" from the voters for presidential leadership tends to make the presidential party more unified and promotes defectors from the opposition party to vote with the president's party. The media has been found to treat new presidents more favorably early in their term than in later years. Public approval of presidential leadership and priorities is generally highest during these early days. Together, these factors create

---

[1] Quoted in Karen O'Conner, et. al., *American Government: Continuity and Change* (New York: Pearson Longman, 2008), p. 304.
[2] Karen O'Conner, et. al., *American Government: Continuity and Change* (New York: Pearson Longman, 2008), p. 304.

what is called the presidential "honeymoon effect" during the First 100 Days.[3]

In studying the presidential honeymoon with Congress, scholars refer to such things as presidential "success rates," presidential "support scores," "party loyalty rates," and "party defection rates." The president's **"success rate"** is the percentage of time Congress supports measures that he has declared a position on. The president's **"support score"** is the percentage of time individual members support a president's policy proposals, and/or the percentage of members of Congress who typically support his ideas. **"Party loyalty rates"** are the percent of presidential party members who stick with their party during hotly contested "party unity" votes, when the majority of one party votes against the majority of the other party. And **"party defection rates"** are the percent of opposing party members who cross over to vote with the president's party during these contested "party unity" votes. All of these rates commonly increase during the First 100 Days, and that is one way that scholars measure and compare different presidential honeymoon periods.

In this exercise, you will become a scholar of the presidential honeymoon (or lack thereof) with Congress. You will explore historic presidential success rates and compare them to the rates of the current president. You will examine just how unified the president's party in Congress is, how often both parties are getting along in supporting the president's leadership, and the extent of defections of opposition party members, who might be voting with the president's party. In the end, you will have gathered the data to judge for yourself whether the new president is enjoying a loving honeymoon with Congress, or is fast on the path to divorce.

---

[3] Casey B. Dominguez, "The President's Honeymoon with Congress: Explaining Reagan's 1981 Victories," WP 2002-3. Institute for Government Studies (UC Berkeley) (2002), http://repositories.cdlib.org/cgi/viewcontent.cgi?article=1003&context=igs (accessed on October 13, 2008).

PRESIDENTIAL SUPPORT IN CONGRESS

1. A key tool for investigating presidential success is what's known as the "presidential success" score: how often does Congress support measures on which the president has expressed an opinion? It is often expected that during the First 100 Days, the "honeymoon effect" will result in a president posting presidential success scores higher than those presidents usually post in non-honeymoon periods.

2. To investigate how presidential success in Congress has varied over time, and how it has changed over the course of each president's term, examine the chart below, which was compiled from data reported in *Congressional Quarterly*. The chart shows how often modern presidents have been successful with Congress, as defined by the percent of times Congress has passed roll-call measures on which the president has expressed an opinion. Study the chart and notice how success rates change, or don't change, over time—also compare the presidents' success rates in their first year of office, compared to later.

Presidential Success Rates in Congress		
	First 100 Days (or First Year, if *)	Last Year	Median Success Rate
Eisenhower	89%*	65%	72%
Kennedy	92%	87%	85%
Johnson	88%*	75%	83%
Nixon	100%	60%	67%
Ford	58.2%*	54%	58%
Carter	80%	75%	76%
Reagan	100%	47%	62%
Bush (H.W.)	40%	43%	52%
Clinton	94%	55%	58%
Bush (W.)	87%*	14%	Unavailable

note: Bush (W.) "last year" data is for 2007

Sources: C. Dominguez, WP2002-3, Inst. for Govt. Studies (UC Berkeley), 2002; *CQ Weekly Report*, January 12, 2000.

3. Can you detect a "honeymoon effect" from the data in this chart (e.g., the tendency for a president to receive more support early in his term than later in his term)? *Use your worksheet to describe the presidential success trends that you notice in this chart, and comment on what you learn about the honeymoon effect.*

4. You can now investigate how well the current president is doing in his Congressional "support" scores, and compare his early scores to the "first year" scores of the presidents in the chart above.

5. Data regarding how often Congress supports measures on which the president has taking a position is not easily available. Some online companies like Congressional Quarterly track this data, but they charge fees to access it. For this exercise, you will access an online database that charges fees for its services—but which you can access for one week, using a free trial.

6. Go to **www.hillmonitor.com**.

7. This website offers an easy way to research Congressional support for measures on which the president has taken a position. But you have to sign up for a free trial to use it. **Click the "Free Trial" button in the menu bar to the right.**

✓ **Stay on top of every bill introduced with BillTracker**

8. A form appears for you to request your free trial. **Fill it out and click "Submit."** You should receive your login information within 24 hours. You cannot complete steps 9–14 until you receive this information, but you can complete steps 15 onward while you are waiting for your password.

9. **When you receive your HillMonitor username and password, use it to logon to www.hillmonitor.com.**

10. After logging on, you will see the Main Menu screen, with many options to explore the data at this site. For this exercise, you are interested in viewing votes on key measures in which the president expressed an opinion. For efficiency purposes, you will only examine votes in the House of Representatives, as opposed to votes in both the House and the Senate. **To see those key House votes, look under the "Report" section of the Main Page, and click on "Key Votes—House."**

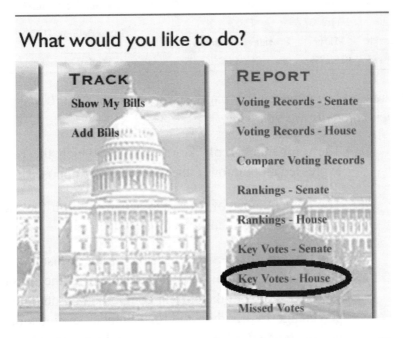

11. A page appears with a list of key votes taken by the current House of Representatives. The president may have taken a position on many of

these key votes, and you can see that information on this page. See the screenshot below for guidance on reading this material.

12. Review all key votes on this page, but no more than 20. *Using scratch paper, calculate the following:*

    a. The total number of "key votes" on which the president expressed an opinion (either in support or opposed)

    b. The total number of times the actual vote on the measure matched the president's opinion

    c. The percent of times that the vote on the measure matched the president's opinion. This percentage is the president's "success score" in the current congress. You determine this percentage by dividing the total number of times the final vote matched the president's opinion by the total number of measures on which the president voiced an opinion (i.e., [b] divided by [a]).

13. *Fill in all these scores on your worksheet.*

14. Compare the president's success rate that you have just determined to the success rate of previous presidents in their first year, as seen in the chart after step 2, on page 131. Is the support score of the current president significantly higher, significantly lower, or about the same as most previous presidents, and what does that suggest about the nature of this president's "honeymoon"? *Fill in this answer in your worksheet.*

15. Other ways to measure the president's success in Congress include*:*

    a. Examining the extent of party loyalty among the president's party (party loyalty is the tendency of members of the party to vote in accordance with the majority of their party on contested measures). *If a presidential honeymoon is having an effect on Congressional votes, we would expect the president's party to demonstrate party loyalty that is higher than average.*

    b. Examining how often a majority of the opposition party's members vote against a majority of the president's party members (these votes are called "party unity" votes). *If a presidential honeymoon is having an effect on Congressional votes, we would expect that the number of polarized votes, where majorities of the two parties line up against each other, will be lower than average, as parties more frequently unite to advance the president's agenda.*

    c. Finally, you can examine how many opposition party members vote **with** the president's party, even when a majority of their party members are **opposed** to the president. This can be called the opposition party's "defection rate." *If a presidential honeymoon is having a significant effect on Congressional votes, we would expect that the number of opposition party members who defect* *from their party to vote with a majority of the president's party will be higher than average.*

16. To review "normal" political tendencies since 1991 on the bulleted points above, review the charts below. In these charts, you can see data for the total number of all votes that were **"Party Unity"** votes, where a majority of one party's members vote against the majority of the other party's members (point a., above). You can also see **"Party Loyalty"** data, showing the tendency of a party's members to stick together in key votes (point b., above). Finally, you can see **"Party Defection"** rates—the percentage of non-presidential party members who defect to "the other side" on these key votes (point c., above).

Roll Call Votes in House of Representatives

Year	% of all Votes That Were Party Unity Votes	Republican Party Loyalty	Democratic Party Loyalty
1991	60.2%	82.1%	86.0%
1993	63.9%	87.2%	88.5%
1995	67.5%	91.8%	83.4%
1997	52.9%	89.6%	85.4%
1999	45.3%	89.3%	86.6%
2001	41.6%	93.4%	87.8%
2003	49.6%	93.7%	90.7%
2005	51.5%	92.3%	90.4%
Average	54.1%	89.9%	87.3%

Average Defection of Republicans to Democratic Side	10.1%
Average Defection of Democrats to Republican Side	12.7%

source: Jeff Lewis and Keith Poole data at
polarizedamerica.com/#POLITICALPOLARIZATION

17. How do these numbers compare with the current Congressional data, during the First 100 Days of the new president? You can conduct research on this question by going to **www.govtrack.us**. This site has excellent resources for tracking current activity in Congress.

18. You are interested in reviewing the data regarding "Roll Call Votes" (votes where the preference of individual members of Congress are recorded). **Scroll down the page to the "Roll Call Votes" button and click it.**

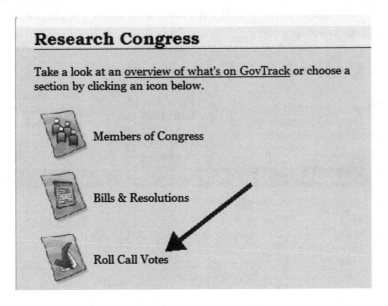

19. You are taken to a "Roll Call Votes" database, which lists the subject of all roll call votes in Congress over the last year and has links to all roll call votes. Using this list, **click on the first 15 roll call votes you see**, following these rules:

   a. Click ONLY on House votes, NOT on Senate votes

   b. DO NOT click on any votes on motions to adjourn

   c. Make sure that each of your "first" 15 roll call votes is for a different date, so as to get votes from a range of dates.

Choosing 15 roll call votes gives you a small sample of votes from which you can calculate "party loyalty" percentages and the like. Clicking on the first 15 votes that you see, according to the rules above, helps ensure that you select a random sample, rather than choosing ones that look most interesting to you. Of course, this sample size is FAR too low to return scientifically valid data, but you begin to see how this kind of research is done, and your data might in fact parallel data found by more complete reviews of this same subject.

20. Scroll through the list of roll call votes and **click on the first of your 15 votes**, following the rules above.

Roll Call Votes Database

Email Print X

The Senate and House each conduct hund[...] each year, used both to pass legislation and amendments as well as to a[...] for quorum calls. Use the options to the left to navigate the voting re[...]

This is a link to a House roll call vote. Click 15 of these kinds of links.

All votes (this year)	
Vote & Date	**Vote Description**
House Roll #683 Oct 3, 2008 2:41 PM	On Passage - House - H.R. 6867 Unemployment Compensation Extension Act of 2008 - Under Suspension of the Rules Passed 368-28, 38 not voting (2/3 required)
House Roll #682 Oct 3, 2008 1:29 PM	On Passage - House - S 3197 National Guard and Reservists Debt Relief A[...] - Under Suspension of the Rules Passed 411-0, 22 not voting (2/3 required)

21. A screen appears with a clear breakdown of exactly how members of each party voted on this measure. You can easily see if this vote should be categorized as a "party unity" vote—which is a vote where a majority of the members of one party vote against a majority of the members of the other party. You can also see the number of party members who "defected" from the majority of their party—and from that number you can calculate "party loyalty" and "party defection" rates. See screenshot on the next page for further guidance.

Vote Number: House Vote #683 in

Date: Oct 3, 2008 2:41PM

Result: Passed

Related Bill: H.R. 6867: Unemp

> Here you see the number of Dems and Reps voting for and against this measure. Here's how you tell if a majority of one party voted against a majority of the other party. On this vote, that wasn't the case—so this wouldn't be called a "Party Unity" vote.

Overview

	Totals	Democrats	Republicans	Independents
Ayes:	368 (85%)	226	142	0
Nays:	28 (6%)	0	28	0
No Vote:	38 (9%)	9	29	0	A)
Required:	2/3 of 396 votes (=264 votes)			

22. Review the data for the first vote you clicked on, and **use scratch paper to record and calculate the following**:

   a. *Was this vote a "party unity vote"?* In other words, did a majority of one party's members vote differently from a majority of the other party's members?

   b. *Calculate a party loyalty score.* If the vote WAS a party unity vote, what was the percent of the president's party members who voted with the majority of that party's members? (You calculate this percentage by dividing the number of party members who voted with the majority of their party by the total number of party members who voted. For example, in the screen shot above, you would divide 142 [Republicans voting with the majority of their party] by 170 [total Republicans voting], to get the Republican party unity score.) If the vote was NOT a party unity vote, ignore this step.

   c. *Calculate a party defection score.* If the vote WAS a party unity vote, what was the percent of the opposition party members (members from the non-presidential party) who defected and voted WITH the majority of presidential party members? You calculate this by dividing the total number of non-presidential members who voted with the majority of the presidential party by the total non-presidential party members who voted. If the vote was NOT a party unity vote, ignore this step.

23. Repeat step 24 for 14 more roll call votes that meet the conditions laid out in step 21.

24. Once you have data on all 15 roll call votes, you can calculate the following:

   a. What *percent* of the 15 votes were party unity votes?

   b. On all party unity votes, what was the *average* party loyalty score of the presidential party?

   c. On all party unity votes, what was the *average* party defection score of the non-presidential party?

25. *Fill this information in on your worksheet, in the chart provided there, which already has the average number of party unity votes, average party loyalty scores, and average party defection scores from previous Congresses, as calculated from the chart that you reviewed in step 16.*

   *The chart also includes a reminder of how your "First 100 Days" data should compare to the historical data of average Congressional behavior, **IF** there is a honeymoon effect during the First 100 Days.*

26. You can tell from this chart whether Congressional voting patterns during the First 100 Days suggest a honeymoon effect or not. Of course, your sample is not large enough for truly scientific conclusions, but what *suggestive* conclusions can you draw from the data in this chart? Or do you conclude that this data is off the mark, due to the small sample size? *Summarize your thoughts on the worksheet.*

Done!

PRESIDENTIAL SUCCESS IN CONGRESS

1. Describe the presidential success trends that you notice in the chart in step 2, and comment on what you learn about the honeymoon effect.

2. Fill in the information below.

Total Key Votes on Which President Expressed an Opinion	
Total Times That Actual Vote Matched the President's Preference	
% of Time That Actual Vote Matched the President's Preference (President's "Success Score")	

3. Is the support score of the current president significantly higher, lower, or about the same as most previous presidents, and what does that suggest about the nature of this president's "honeymoon"?

4. Fill in the information below.

	Percent of All Votes That are Party-Unity Votes	Average Presidential Party Loyalty Rate on Party-Unity Votes	Average Non-Presidential Party Defection Rate on Party-Unity Votes
Historic Averages, 1991–2006	54.1%	88.2%	10.9%
Your First 100 Days Data			
If there is a honeymoon effect, how should your data compare to historic/average data?	Your data should be lower as party-line votes should decline, as the president brings the parties together.	Your data should be higher, as the president's party becomes exceptionally unified.	Your data should be higher, as the opposition party loses an abnormally high number of voters to the president's party.

5. What *suggestive* conclusions can you draw from the data in this completed chart? Or do you conclude that this data is completely off the mark, due to the small sample size?

"Stroke of the pen. Law of the Land. Kind of cool." That is how former Clinton advisor, Paul Begala, described the process of presidential policy-making through Executive Orders.[1] Begala's quote highlights the fact that presidents don't only rule by working with Congress to pass news laws. In fact, a good deal of presidential power has nothing to do with passing laws—for example, presidents can shape policy and put their imprint on society by issuing Executive Orders without any Congressional support, or by delivering persuasive speeches from the presidential "bully pulpit."

Though James Madison argued in Federalist Paper # 47 that America did not need to worry about presidential tyranny because the president "cannot of himself make a law," the reality is that presidents over the years have effectively gained law-making powers in the form of Executive Orders. The Supreme Court once said the president was not meant to be a "lawmaker" and stepped in to repudiate President Truman's Executive Order instructing the government to take over American steel companies (*Youngstown Sheet and Tube v. Sawyer,* 1952). Still, this was a rare decision, and the general rule has been for both Congress and the Court to accept the president's expanding use of Executive Orders.

Executive Orders can be described as "legally binding orders given by the President, acting as the head of the executive branch, to federal administrative agencies. . . . Executive Orders do not require Congressional approval to take effect but they have the same legal weight as laws passed by Congress."[2] Executive Orders include ceremonial proclamations (such as President George W. Bush's declaration of a "Marriage Protection Week"), National Security Directives, and domestic policy directives. Presidents have used Executive Orders to order desegregation of the armed forces, schools and housing. President Reagan used an Executive Order to bar doctors using federal funds to talk about abortion. President Clinton

---

[1] Quoted in James Bennett, "True to Form, Clinton Shifts Energies Back to U.S. Focus." *The New York Times* (July 5, 1998).

[2] Jeffrey C. Fox, "What Is an Executive Order?" www.thisnation.com/question/040.html (accessed on October 6, 2008).

designated millions of acres as a national monument with an Executive Order. President George W. Bush established a program of "faith-based" social services with an Executive Order.

In their First 100 Days, presidents can make a quick impact by issuing Executive Orders, rather than waiting on the slow and contentious process of Congressional law-making to get things done. For example, President Franklin Roosevelt used Executive Orders quickly to "take over" the nation's banking system and begin reorganizing the economy as a response to the Great Depression. President Reagan used Executive Orders to deregulate oil and petroleum production and revoked wage and price control programs immediately upon taking office. President Clinton quickly reversed a ban on federal dollars being used to talk about abortion.

Another form of presidential leadership that does not rely on law-making is what President Roosevelt called the "bully pulpit"—by which he meant that presidents have power, through their speeches, to focus national energies and catalyze action. President Kennedy's optimistic talk about civic service and national mission fueled youth civic engagement and brought the nation together around the mission to send a man to the moon. President Reagan famously demanded the Soviet Union to "tear down this wall" (the Berlin Wall), fueling pressures that ultimately resulted in the wall coming down. Here's how President Reagan described the power of speech-making to unite and mobilize the nation around the moral vision and priorities of the president: "Theodore Roosevelt said that the presidency is a bully pulpit—the pulpit is where the clergyman preaches sermons. It is that. I think this office does offer an opportunity for mobilizing public sentiment behind worthwhile causes."[3]

In this exercise, you will explore two "non-legislative" forms of presidential power: Executive Orders and the bully pulpit. You will explore how Executive Orders have been used in history, and how that compares to the trends of the current president. You will also review a few of the public speeches of the current president and reflect on how those speeches can be considered a form of presidential leadership.

---

[3] Quoted in William Ker Muir, *The Bully Pulpit.* (San Francisco: ICS Press, 1992), p. 7.

EXECUTIVE ORDERS AND THE BULLY PULPIT

1. One way that presidents lead without actually passing new laws is to issue an Executive Order, as described in the introduction to this exercise. To gain historical understanding of the importance of such orders through American history—and of the way in which such orders allow presidents to lead in new policy directions, even without the consent of Congress—you can review some of the more important Executive Orders in history.

2. In 1803, President Jefferson acted without prior Congressional approval, and with unclear constitutional authority, to announce an Executive Order that has changed the course of American history like no other (though it wasn't called "Executive Order" at the time). To see what President Jefferson announced in his accord, without prior involvement by Congress, go to **www.archives.gov/exhibits/american_originals/louistxt.html**.

3. *What was Jefferson's historic "Executive Order"? Provide the answer on your worksheet.*

4. Another sweeping Executive Order that would remake the course of American history was issued by President Lincoln in 1862. In issuing this order, President Lincoln did not have the support of Congress. He also was directly repudiating a Supreme Court decision (Dred Scott), which concluded that the federal government had no authority to do what Lincoln actually did in this 1862 Executive Order. To see the order, go to **www.pbs.org/wgbh/aia/part4/4h1549t.html**.

5. *What was Lincoln's historic Executive Order? Provide the answer on your worksheet.*

6. Franklin Roosevelt issued more Executive Orders than any other president, as a response to the Great Depression and to the challenges of World War II. One Executive Order, issued on February 19, 1942,

deprived thousands of American citizens of their constitutional rights and is remembered as a low point in American history. To view some material surrounding Executive Order 9066, go to **www.pbs.org/ childofcamp/history/eo9066.html.**

7. *What was the subject of Franklin Roosevelt's Executive Order 9066? Provide the answer on your worksheet.*

8. President Truman issued a historic Executive Order that was later overturned by the Supreme Court—one of only two Executive Orders to ever be repudiated by the Court. Truman's order 10340, issued in 1952, was meant to foster stability in the economy and help the American war effort in Korea. To see the text of Executive Order 10340, go to **http://steelseizure.stanford.edu/exec.order10340.html**.

9. *What was the subject of Truman's Executive Order 10340? Provide the answer on your worksheet.*

10. In 1957, President Eisenhower used an Executive Order to authorize federal troops to occupy territory in Arkansas in order to enforce orders of the federal courts that were being resisted in that state. To view Eisenhower's order for federal troops to deploy "within the State of Arkansas to serve in the active military service of the United States for an indefinite period and until relieved by appropriate orders," go to **www.africanamericans.com/ExecutiveOrder10730.htm**.

11. *What was the subject of Eisenhower's Executive Order 10730? Provide the answer on your worksheet.*

12. You have now reviewed some of the most important Executive Orders in American history. Now you will look over a few recent Executive Orders, from the Clinton and George W. Bush presidencies. The National Archives of the Federal Government maintains an online record of all Executive Orders since 1937. Go to the archives at **www.archives.gov/federal-register/executive-orders/.**

13. On this "Executive Orders" page, you can see options to explore this subject. For this exercise, you are interested in the list of Executive Orders, broken down by president, that appears when you click the link for **"Executive Orders Disposition Tables"** (see screenshot).

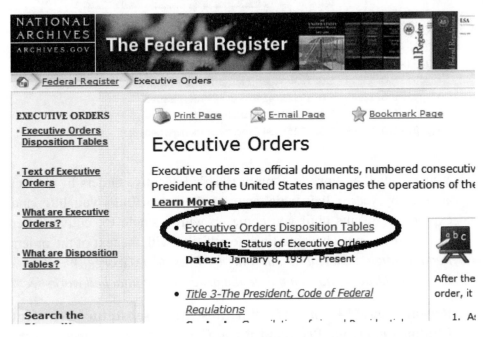

14. When you click on the **Executive Orders Disposition Tables** link, a page loads with all the presidents' names since Franklin Roosevelt. You can click on any of these names to see options to search for the Executive Orders they issued during their presidency. **Click on George W. Bush's name to see his Executive Order list.**

Administration of George W. Bush (2001-Present)

Disposition of Executive orders signed by President George W. Bush:

- Subject Index — *Click here for an alphabetic list of searchable subjects*

- 2008 - E.O. 13454 - E.O. 13466 (13 Executive orders issued)
- 2007 - E.O. 13422 - E.O. 13453 (31 Executive orders issued)
- 2006 - E.O. 13395 - E.O. 1342~~~~
- 2005 — E.O. ~~~~ — *Click here to see a list of orders issued in any given year*
- 2004 - E.O. 13324 - E.O. 1336~~
- 2003 - E.O. 13283 - E.O. 13323 (41 Executive orders issued)
- 2002 - E.O. 13252 - E.O. 13282 (31 Executive orders issued)
- 2001 - E.O. 13198 - E.O. 13251 (54 Executive orders issued)

15. You can click on links to explore Bush's Executive Orders by subject area, or by year. **Click whichever of these two links you like**, and explore the results until you come up with a single Executive Order that interests you. There are links to pdf files with the text of the orders. *Read enough material about one of President George W. Bush's Executive Orders and summarize the order on the attached worksheet.*

16. **Repeat steps 14 and 15, but this time substitute President Clinton's name for President Bush**. *Fill out your worksheet with the information for President Clinton.*

17. Information from this same website allows you to research a wide variety of interesting questions about the use of Executive Orders over time. For example, you can compare which presidents used Executive Orders the most and the least, and you can draw conclusions about whether presidents are using Executive Orders more in modern times than they did in previous decades.

18. Return to the "Executive Orders Disposition Tables" page that lists the clickable names of all the presidents. This is the page you visited in steps 12–14 above, and it is located at **www.archives.gov/federal-register/executive-orders/disposition.html**.

19. When you click a president's name, a screenshot like the following one appears. For each president, you can see information regarding the total number of Executive Orders issued (at the bottom of the page), and the number of Executive Orders issued in each year. The screen shot arrows show you where to look for this information.

Administration of George Bush (1989-1993)

Disposition of Executive orders signed by President George Bush:

- <u>1989</u> - E.O. 12668 - E.O. 12698 (31 Executive orders signed)
- <u>1990</u> - E.O. 12699 - E.O. 12741 (43 Executive orders signed)
- <u>1991</u> - E.O. 12742 - E.O. 12787 (46 Executive orders signed)
- <u>1992</u> - E.O. 12788 - E.O. 12827 (40 Executive orders signed)
- <u>1993</u> - E.O. 12828 - E.O. 12833 (6 Executive orders signed)

<u>Bush Presidentia Library & Museum</u>

166 Total Executive Orders Issued ◀

20. By clicking on various presidents' names, determine the total number of Executive Orders issued by each of six presidents (listed below). Also determine the number of Executive Orders issued during each of these president's **first year in office**—a period of time overlapping with, but going beyond, the First 100 Days period you are studying in this workbook. Determine the total Executive Orders issued and the total orders in the first year in office for three presidents who served more than 50 years ago (Franklin Roosevelt, Truman and Eisenhower) and for the three most recent presidents, George H. W. Bush, Bill Clinton and George W. Bush. *Fill in the information on your worksheet.*

21. Based on what you have learned about three presidencies from 50 years ago, and three presidencies in the last 15 years, do you conclude that modern presidents are becoming **more** or **less** likely to utilize Executive Orders to govern, when compared to earlier presidents? *Fill in the answer on your worksheet.*

22. You are now ready to look at some of the specific Executive Orders that the new president has issued in his first months in office. Return to the "Executive Orders Disposition Tables" page that lists the clickable

names of all the presidents. This is the page you visited in steps 13, 14 and 18 above, and it is located at **www.archives.gov/federal-register/executive-orders/disposition.html**.

23. On this page, click on the name of the current president to see a list of Executive Orders issued by the new president. Just as you did with President George W. Bush and President Clinton, explore some Executive Orders, reading titles and browsing through the text of the orders. *When you are done, pick two Executive Orders that you find interesting and summarize them on the worksheet.*

24. If the new president maintains the same pace of Executive Orders throughout the entire year, will he have issued about the same number of Executive Orders during his first year as Clinton and Bush (you found data on Clinton and Bush in step 20), or will he have issued significantly more or fewer Executive Orders? To calculate the answer, you have to multiply the existing Executive Orders of the new president by 4 if you are doing this exercise in mid-late April, by 3 if you are doing it in May, and by 6 if you are doing it in early April or earlier. *Enter the answer on your worksheet.*

25. What reason can you offer as to why the new president's use of Executive Orders seems to either parallel the recent historic pattern, or as to why Executive Orders are growing or shrinking considerably? *Fill in your thoughts on your worksheet.*

26. Another important way that a president leads without signing laws is through the power of the "bully pulpit." At the turn of the century, President Theodore Roosevelt called the White House a "bully pulpit," by which he meant that presidents could lead through the power of public speeches, which the public and the media pay close attention to. You can research how the new president is using this power because the White House makes almost all public speeches of the president available online. To see them, go to the National Archives of the Federal Register at **www.archives.gov/federal-register/**.

27. The Office of the Federal Register provides access to presidential documents like public speeches. Scroll down this page and look for a section titled **"From the White House."** In that section, click a a link titled **"Weekly Compilation of Presidential Documents."**

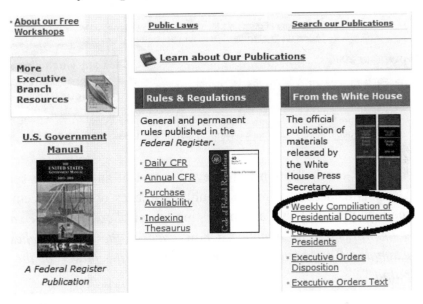

28. On the page that follows, click the option to see documents as **"an electronic publication, free of charge, of the GPO Access Service."**

29. You will be taken to the main page of the "Weekly Compilation of Presidential Documents." You will see search boxes giving you the ability to search documents from years past. To see some of the documents of the current president, **click the "GO" button next to the option to browse documents from 2001 to 2009.** See screenshot for the button you want.

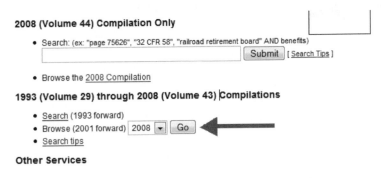

30. On the page that follows, presidential documents (e.g., the text of public speeches) are organized by week. **Click on any week since the new president was inaugurated** and a list of public pronouncements and speeches given by the president during that week appears.

January | February | March | April | May | June | July August | September | October | November | December

September 2008

- September 29, 2008 — Volume 44, Number 38 (
- September 25, 2008 — Volume 44, Number 37 (Page
- September 15, 2008 — Volume 44, Number 36 (Pages
- September 8, 2008 — Volume 44, Number 35 (Pages: 1167-1178)
- September 1, 2008 — Volume 44, Number 34 (Pages: 1153-1166)

Click any week since the new president was inaugurated

31. You will see the option to retrieve the text of any of those speeches. Use this database to find two public speeches or pronouncements of the new president that are interesting to you. *Look them over and use your worksheet to summarize how each of the two speeches is an example of presidential leadership through the power of the "bully pulpit."*

32. You have begun to research presidential leadership through tools other than lawmaking. For a full picture of the president's success in non-legislative leadership, you would need to look over a wider range of pronouncements and Executive Orders. Other forms of leadership without lawmaking would include the president's appointment power, such as his appointments to important bureaucratic positions and his appointments to the Federal Courts and Supreme Court. You will not have time to explore these other dynamics in this exercise, but you have built a bit of a foundation for understanding the importance of non-legislative forms of presidential power.

Done!

EXECUTIVE ORDERS AND THE BULLY PULPIT

1. What was President Jefferson's historic "Executive Order"?

2. What was President Lincoln's historic Executive Order?

3. What was President Franklin Roosevelt's historic Executive Order?

4. What was President Truman's historic Executive Order?

5. What was President Eisenhower's historic Executive Order?

6. Describe the President Bush Executive Order that you reviewed.

7. Describe the President Clinton Executive Order that you reviewed.

8. Fill in the information below.

President's Name	Total Executive Orders	Executive Orders in First Year
Franklin Roosevelt		
Harry Truman		
Dwight Eisenhower		
George H.W. Bush		
Bill Clinton		
George W. Bush		

9. Are modern presidents more or less likely to issue Executive Orders than presidents of fifty years ago?

10. Summarize one Executive Order issued by the new president.

11. Summarize a second Executive Order issued by the new president.

12. If the new president maintains this pace of Executive Orders throughout his first year, will he generally equal the number of Executive Orders issued by President Bush and President Clinton in their first year, or will his orders be significantly higher or lower?

13. What reason(s) can you offer as to why the new president's use of Executive Orders seems to be roughly the same, or higher or lower, than recent previous presidents?

14. What was the president speaking about in the first speech or pronouncement you reviewed, and how is this speech an example of presidential leadership?

15. What was the president speaking about in the second speech or pronouncement you reviewed, and how is this speech an example of presidential leadership?

ISSUE TWELVE: LOOKING BACKWARD
ASSESSING THE FIRST 100 DAYS

The First 100 Days has been called "the defining moment" for a new president,[1] "the standard by which [all] administrations are judged,"[2] and "the new president's first and perhaps best chance to reshape the nation according to his own agenda and vision."[3] Presidents from FDR forward have promised significant progress during their First 100 Days while campaigning, have used the First 100 Days as a personal milestone, and have held special media events on the anniversary of their hundredth day in office. Scholars have found that presidential power is a fleeting thing, and that a president's political capital and national popularity tend to decline over time, so it is vital to hit the ground running from the time a president takes office. According to presidential advisor H. R. Haldeman, "You've got the power now, don't listen to anyone else. Your power is going to start eroding from January 20th on."[4]

Through the exercises in this workbook, you have witnessed firsthand the new president's strategies, and his success or lack thereof, in making the most of his First 100 Days. You have witnessed how the inaugural address was received, have explored whether the president truly has a "mandate" to lead, and have studied the lessons in the way the president built his cabinet and his budget. You investigated relationships between the president and the people, the president and the press, and the president and the Planet. You learned more about unique presidential tools, such as Executive Orders, executive agreements, and the bully pulpit.

---

[1] Jonathan Alter, *The Defining Moment: FDR's Hundred Days and the Triumph of Hope* (Simon and Schuster: New York, 2006).
[2] "Looking Back: FDR's 100 First Days." *The Nation* (n.d.), www.thenation.com/classroom/paks/pakFDRs_first_hundred_days.mhtml (accessed October 15, 2008).
[3] William Lasser, "Just How Critical Are the First 100 Days?" (n.d.) http://college.cengage.com/polisci/resources/first_100_days/articles/critical.html (accessed on October 15, 2008).
[4] Quoted in James Pfiffner, *The Strategic Presidency* (Chicago: Dorsey Press, 1988), p. 7.

Now it is time to come to some final assessments about the meaning of the First 100 Days for this president. FDR's First 100 Days are remembered as a grand success, restoring hope and energy to the American people—while George W. Bush's First 100 Days are generally found to be forgettable. How will we remember the First 100 Days of the current president?

In this final exercise, you will explore this question by reviewing some current assessments in the national media. As a unique window into the national mood, you will also explore how editorial cartoonists portray the early days of presidential terms, from FDR to Bush to the current president. Finally, you will review some promises that the current president made concerning his First 100 Days while he was running for election. Has the president lived up to these early promises?

It is time to look backward at the 100-day journey of the new president and the American people and to assess just what it has all meant.

ASSESSING THE FIRST 100 DAYS

1. Since the historic presidency of FDR, there has been a national obsession with assessing and evaluating the First 100 Days of all new presidents. Your first step in assessing the First 100 Days of the new president will be briefly to review some of the ways the "First 100 Days" frame has been used to guide assessments of past presidencies.

2. It all started with Franklin Roosevelt's "First 100 Days." Following FDR's burst of legislation in his First 100 Days after taking office during the Great Depression, newspapers across the country used the "First 100 Days" frame to evaluate how he was doing. Some of the most famous editorials were run in *The Nation*, an influential journal of the time. To review one of those editorials, go to **www.thenation. com/classroom/paks/pakFDRs_first_hundred_days.mhtml**.

3. **Read the editorial that you find there.** What is the overall tone of the editorial? Did the author feel FDR was doing a good or poor job of governing during this First 100 Days? *Summarize the tone on your worksheet.*

4. Now you will compare the editorial coverage of FDR's First 100 Days to the kind of evaluations George W. Bush received for his First 100 Days. You will read only one editorial—but it is representative of the tone of much of the coverage of the Bush administration. Go to **www.brookings.edu/opinions/2001/0601governance_light.aspx**.

5. **Read the editorial that you find there.** What is the overall tone of the editorial? Did the author feel Bush was doing a good or poor job of governing during his First 100 Days? *Summarize the tone on your worksheet.*

6. You can see from these editorials, and from the material in issue one of this workbook, that there is no avoiding the "First 100 Days" frame, in terms of evaluating the performance of a new president. This same "First 100 Days" frame has even shaped the behavior and evaluations

159

of Congress. As Democratic Representative Nancy Pelosi (CA) was leading her party toward claiming majority power in Congress in the 2006 elections, she urged voters to take faith from the "100 *Hours*" agenda that her party was offering the people—a clear reference to the "First 100 Days" frame that people are so familiar with. To review Pelosi's use of this frame, go to **www.huffingtonpost.com/rep-nancy-pelosi/one-hundred-hours b 33529.html**. You can read a short editorial by Speaker Nancy Pelosi about her "100 Hours Agenda."

7. You should be doing this exercise at the very end of April or in early May, which is the conclusion of the current president's First 100 Days in office. Therefore, you can review some of the inevitable reporting on how the First 100 Days has gone for the current president.

8. **Conduct a simple Google search for news editorials and similar analysis of the First 100 Days of the current presidency.** Use such search terms as "First 100 Days + [name of current president]." When the list of results appears, try to locate mainstream and reputable editorials/analyses from such sources as the *New York Times*, the *Washington Post*, the *Wall Street Journal*, CNN, PBS or NPR— though you may review any analysis on the subject that interests you. **Follow the links to review at least TWO evaluations of the First 100 Days of the current president.** These evaluations might be a newspaper editorial, a print news report, a television news report, a reporters' roundtable, or the like.

9. What do you learn about how the current president's First 100 Days performance is being assessed? *Summarize what you learn on the worksheet.*

10. Presidents' performances are evaluated through news reporting—but they are also evaluated through editorial cartoons, which have a long history of commenting on the political affairs in America. Your next

step will be to compare the editorial cartoons commenting on FDR's First 100 Days to the cartoons commenting on George W. Bush's early days. Then you will examine how the current president is being portrayed by the cartoonists.

11. Begin by going to **http://xroads.virginia.edu/~ma02/volpe/newdeal/ cartoons.html**.

12. You see a collection of editorial cartoons from the Roosevelt presidency. Scroll down this page and you will see a section of cartoons in a section called "Hundred Days." **Review the cartoons you see in this section (click on a cartoon to enlarge it).**

13. What is the overall tone of these editorial cartoons that comment on Roosevelt's early leadership? Choose one cartoon that well represents the overall tone of the group. *Provide the name of the cartoon on your worksheet and summarize the general tone that this cartoon takes on the Roosevelt presidency.*

14. Now you will review how George W. Bush was treated by the editorial cartoonists early in his presidency. Go to **www.amureprints.com**. You are at a site that lets you view cartoons of all sorts over the years.

15. To find cartoons commenting on the early days of the Bush presidency, begin by clicking the **"Advanced Search"** link that is on the bottom of the search box that appears on this home page.

Search For Cartoons and Comics

1) Select a Comic Feature:

All Searchable Features ▾

2) Enter Search Term(s):

Search tips: You can enter more than one keyword. Use "and", "or" or "not" to refine your search. Your keyword will search dialog, captions, descriptions and topics.

Search

Use the Advanced Search for category, date, and Sunday-only search options.

16. A page loads where you can build a search for cartoons commenting on the early days of the Bush presidency. Fill out this search form as follows (see screenshot on next page for how your search form should end up looking):

- Enter "Bush" as the Keyword.

- Leave the default highlighted in the "Feature(s) to Search" box (the default is "All Searchable Features").

- In the "Release Dates" section, type 04/20/2001 in the "From" box, and type 05/05/2001 in the "To" box. You are instructing the system to return only the Bush cartoons that ran from April 20, 2001 to May 5, 2001—a period of time covering the conclusion of Bush's First 100 Days in office.

- In the "Topic Terms" section, highlight "Politics and government."

Keyword(s):

Bush

Search tips: Use AND, OR, AND NOT between keywords. Use * to indicate a wild
example: graduat* will find graduate, graduates, and graduation.

Feature(s) to Search

All Searchable Features
- Comic Features -
Adam@Home
Baldo
Big Top
Boondocks
Borgman, Jim
Calvin & Hobbes
Cathy
Cleats

Search tip: To select more than one feature, hold down the Control key (PC) o
(Mac) and click on the desired feature names.

Release Dates:

From: 04/20/2001   To: 05/05/2001

Search tip: Use format mm/dd/yy

Topic Terms

Health & medicine
Hobbies & handicrafts
Holidays
Home & garden
Hunting & Fishing
Law & legal issues
Literature
Media
Military
Music
Nature
Occupations & employment
Organizations
People
Politics & government

17. When you are done filling in the search form, make sure the option to
"View Images" is selected (bottom of the form) and then click the
"Search" button on the bottom of the form.

18. Several pages of editorial cartoons on the Bush administration should appear. These cartoons all ran near the end of Bush's First 100 Days in office, back in 2001. **Review several of these cartoons**, being sure to click the page links in the top half of your page to move through different pages of cartoon results.

NOTE: This system sometimes returns "NO" search results, even though there are cartoons in the system that ran during this time frame. If you receive a "no search results" message, try expanding the search dates by a few weeks (e.g., input search dates from 04/01/2001 to 05/15/2001). You can then narrow the dates back down, if you like, and redo the search.

19. *Describe the overall tone of the editorial cartoons concerning the Bush administration on your worksheet.*

20. Select one of the Bush cartoons that represents this tone and save it to your desktop (right-click the image and select "save image as," or use any other method to save that you are familiar with). *Now print the image, and attach it to your worksheet.*

21. Now you can review the kind of editorial cartoons that are being run concerning the current president. **Conduct a simple Google IMAGE Search, using the following search terms: "editorial + cartoon + [name of current president]."** You will see a host of cartoons appear.

22. **Review some of these cartoons**, and especially try to find cartoons that have run recently, rather than very early in the new president's term. Based on your review, identify ONE tone or theme (either positive or negative) that seems to reappear in these cartoons. *Summarize that theme on your worksheet.*

23. Select one of the cartoons on the new president that represents this tone or theme and save it to your desktop (right-click the image and select "save image as," or use any other method to save that you are familiar with). *Now print the image, and attach it to your worksheet.*

24. Your final step will be to review some of the new president's own promises and expectations for his First 100 Days that were made during the campaign—and then to assess how well those expectations were met.

If Barack Obama is president, complete ONLY steps 25–28.

If John McCain is president, complete ONLY steps 29–32.

25. Back while Barack Obama was running for the Democratic nomination, he told a Denver audience what he would do during his First 100 Days as president. To view what he had to say, go to **www.youtube.com/watch?v=aaoP6JjsF38**.

26. To supplement this video, or in case this video no longer is present, you can also review what Obama had to say on the subject of his First 100 Days during an interview with *Readers Digest* back during his campaign for the Democratic nomination. Go to **www.rd.com/your-america-inspiring-people-and-stories/interview-with-barack-obama/article45737-1.html**.

27. The question at the very top of the page that loads is "What would the first 100 days of an Obama presidency look like?" **Read Obama's answer to that question.**

28. Based on what you learn in steps 25–27, what were some key "promises" or expectations about his First 100 Days that Obama offered as he was running for office? Do you think that Obama has done a good job in meeting those promises/expectations so far? *Summarize your conclusions on the worksheet.*

29. Back while John McCain was running for the Republican nomination, he told a "town hall" audience some of what he would do during his First 100 Days as president. To view what he had to say, go to **www.youtube.com/watch?v=AljN1aIut2o**.

30. To supplement this video, or in case this video no longer is present, you can also review a speech given by the former CEO of eBay to the 2008 Republican National Convention. To find this speech by Meg Whitman, go to **www.politico.com/news/stories/0908/13135.html**.

31. The text of the speech is there. You don't need to read the entire speech. Around the middle of the speech, Meg Whitman begins to talk about what John McCain would do as president during his First 100 Days. Look for a section of the speech that begins with the following sentence: "In its first 100 days, a McCain administration will put this nation on a path toward energy independence." **Read the next several paragraphs of the speech that follows from this point.**

32. Based on what you learn in steps 29–31, what were some key "promises" or expectations about his First 100 Days that McCain offered as he was running for office? Do you think that McCain has done a good job in meeting those promises/expectations so far? *Summarize your conclusions on the worksheet.*

Done!

ASSESSING THE FIRST 100 DAYS

1. What is the overall tone of the editorial on FDR's First 100 Days?

2. What is the overall tone of the editorial on Bush's First 100 Days?

3. What is the overall tone of the editorials that you read concerning the current president's First 100 Days in office?

4. Provide the name of the FDR cartoon you found interesting and summarize the tone that the cartoons take on the FDR presidency.

5. What is the overall tone of the cartoons on the Bush presidency?

6. Identify one theme or explain the general tone that reappears in several cartoons related to the current president.

7. Has the president adequately met his First 100 Day promises and expectations that he himself laid out in the materials you reviewed? Overall, how do you rate the First 100 Days of the president?

ISSUE ONE: THE FIRST 100 DAYS IN PRESIDENTIAL HISTORY

1. Why is it so important for a president to achieve substantial success in his First 100 Days?

2. Journalist Haynes Johnson says the First 100 Days standard is "a foolish standard to apply to any president." Do you agree?

3. How do you think the current president's First 100 Days will compare to other famous First 100 Day periods, like those of Franklin Roosevelt and Ronald Reagan?

ISSUE TWO: WAS THERE A MANDATE?

1. How can a president ever claim a "mandate," when voters are usually ignorant about the policy goals of candidates, campaigns are driven by simplistic 30-second ads, and the results of the election are usually ambiguous as signals of voters' top concerns?

2. What were the key issues and voter groups in this election?

3. Does the current president have a "mandate" to lead?

ISSUE THREE: ANALYZING THE PRESIDENTIAL INAUGURAL ADDRESS

1. All inaugurals include "obligatory rhetoric." Why?

2. Did the president's inaugural express a coherent theory of proper government and the good society? If so, what was it?

3. Was this a great inaugural address? Why or why not?

ISSUE FOUR: LESSONS OF THE PRESIDENTIAL CABINET

1. What kinds of policies, political groups or ideologies do you expect to benefit from the president's new cabinet?

2. Some cabinet members are arguably appointed partly to represent underrepresented groups in American politics—such as minorities and women. Is it important and wise for presidents to make such calculations in appointing their cabinet?

3. Are you confident in the president's new cabinet?

ISSUE FIVE: EXAMINING PRESIDENTIAL BUDGET PRIORITIES

1. What political priorities does the new president's budget reveal?

2. How does the new budget differ from recent presidential budgets?

3. How will "mandatory" and "discretionary" spending patterns change in the president's new budget?

ISSUE SIX: THE PRESIDENT AND THE PUNDITS

1. First impressions matter. What is the tone of early media coverage of the new president: positive, negative, or what?

2. Do you think that the overall thrust of media coverage of the president reflects a liberal or conservative bias? Or is the press balanced?

3. How can members of the press best serve American democracy in how they report on the president during the First 100 Days? Is the press serving that purpose well?

ISSUE SEVEN: THE PRESIDENT AND THE PLANET

1. What was the general state of world opinion concerning America and its president (George W. Bush) BEFORE the 2008 election? How has world opinion changed, if at all, since the election?

2. What do you think accounts for the ways in which America and its president are perceived across the world?

3. Should Americans be concerned with the country's (or the president's) international reputation? Why or why not?

ISSUE EIGHT: THE PRESIDENT AND THE PEOPLE

1. Why do you think that public approval of a new president tends to be very high during the "honeymoon period"?

2. Why do you think almost all presidents tend to be far less popular when they end their presidency than when they began it?

3. Should presidents pay close attention to their standing in opinion polls? What are the benefits and disadvantages of doing so?

ISSUE NINE: NEW PRESIDENT, NEW FOREIGN POLICY?

1. Presidents have perhaps their greatest ability to shape national policy in the realm of foreign policy. Why is that?

2. What new foreign policy directions, if any, does the president seem to be signaling or pursuing?

3. Executive Agreements allow the president to shape foreign policy without Congressional approval. Should Congress work to restrict this power, which is not mentioned in the Constitution?

ISSUE TEN: PRESIDENTIAL SUPPORT IN CONGRESS

1. Is the president's party showing more or less unity than the opposition party? What does your answer suggest about the state of current politics and the existence of a "honeymoon period"?

2. Is the president enjoying a "honeymoon" with the current Congress? What is the evidence for or against a "honeymoon"?

3. Should members of Congress show the president more deference and support during his first year in office? Why or why not?

ISSUE ELEVEN: LEADING WITHOUT LAWS

1. Should presidents be allowed to create new policies by unilaterally issuing executive orders? How might politics change for the better or worse if Congress had to approve all executive orders?

2. What is the "bully pulpit"? Has the current president made good use of this unique presidential power?

3. In general, is it better to have a very strong or a weak president?

ISSUE TWELVE: ASSESSING THE FIRST 100 DAYS

1. Has the president done a good job of living up to his earlier promises of what he would work on and achieve during the First 100 Days?

2. Do you think that less "serious" media, such as editorial cartoons or satirical shows like Jon Stewart's *The Daily Show*, have a significant effect in shaping national opinion of the president?

3. Overall, did the president have a successful First 100 Days?

SCREENSHOT CREDITS

p. 3: www.fdrlibrary.marist.edu/100home.html

p. 5: www.pbs.org/wgbh/amex/reagan/timeline/index_3.html

p. 7–8: www.pbs.org/newshour/media/100days

p. 9: www.cnn.com/SPECIALS/2001/bush.100/

p. 16–17: www.presidency.ucsb.edu. American Presidency Project.

p. 21–23: www.cnn.com/ELECTION/2004/pages/results/states/US/P/00/

p. 24: www.pollingreport.com. Copyright © 2008, Polling Report Inc.

p. 35–37: www.presidentialrhetoric.com. Design copyright © Paul Stob. Used with permission.

p. 47: http://www.whitehouse.gov/government/cabinet.html

p. 53: www.votesmart.org

p. 53–54: http://www.cnn.com/video

p. 63: www.cbo.gov

p. 64–67: www.gpoaccess.gov/usbudget

p. 68–69: www.heritage.org/Research/Features/

p. 70: www.presidency.ucsb.edu/sou.php. American Presidency Project.

p. 71–72: www.cbo.gov

p. 81: www.mediaresearch.org. © Media Research Center.

p. 82: http://mediamatters.org.

p. 83: www.cmpa.com

p. 84: www.cnn.com

p. 89: www.pbs.org/frontlineworld/ election2008/

p. 90: www.theworld.org/?q=node/21043. © PRI-s The World.

p. 91: http://pewglobal.org

p. 92: www.worldpublicopinion.org. Courtesy of Program on International Policy Attitudes.

p. 101: www.ropercenter.uconn.edu. Copyright held by The Roper Center for Public Opinion Research.

p. 103: www.presidency.ucsb.edu/data/popularity.php. American Presidency Project.

p. 104: www.pollingreport.com. Copyright © 2008, Polling Report Inc.

p. 113: www.thechicagocouncil.org

p. 116: http://www.state.gov/s/l/treaty/

p. 118: www.state.gov/s/l/treaty/caseact/

p. 119: http://www.state.gov/s/l/treaty/caseact/. Used by permission.

p. 120–2: www.stimson.org.fopo. Used by permission

p. 123: www.gpoaccess.gov/wcomp

p. 132–4: www.hillmonitor.com

p. 137–9: www.govtrack.us

p. 147–9: www.archives.gov/federal-register/executive-orders/

p. 151–2: www.archives.gov/federal-register

p. 162: www.amureprints.com.